THIS BOOK BELONGS TO

· · · · · · · · · · · · · · · · · · · · · · · · · · · ·

# ROYAL MANDALA

## Volume 1

### COLORING BOOK COMPILATION OF STUDENT DESIGNS

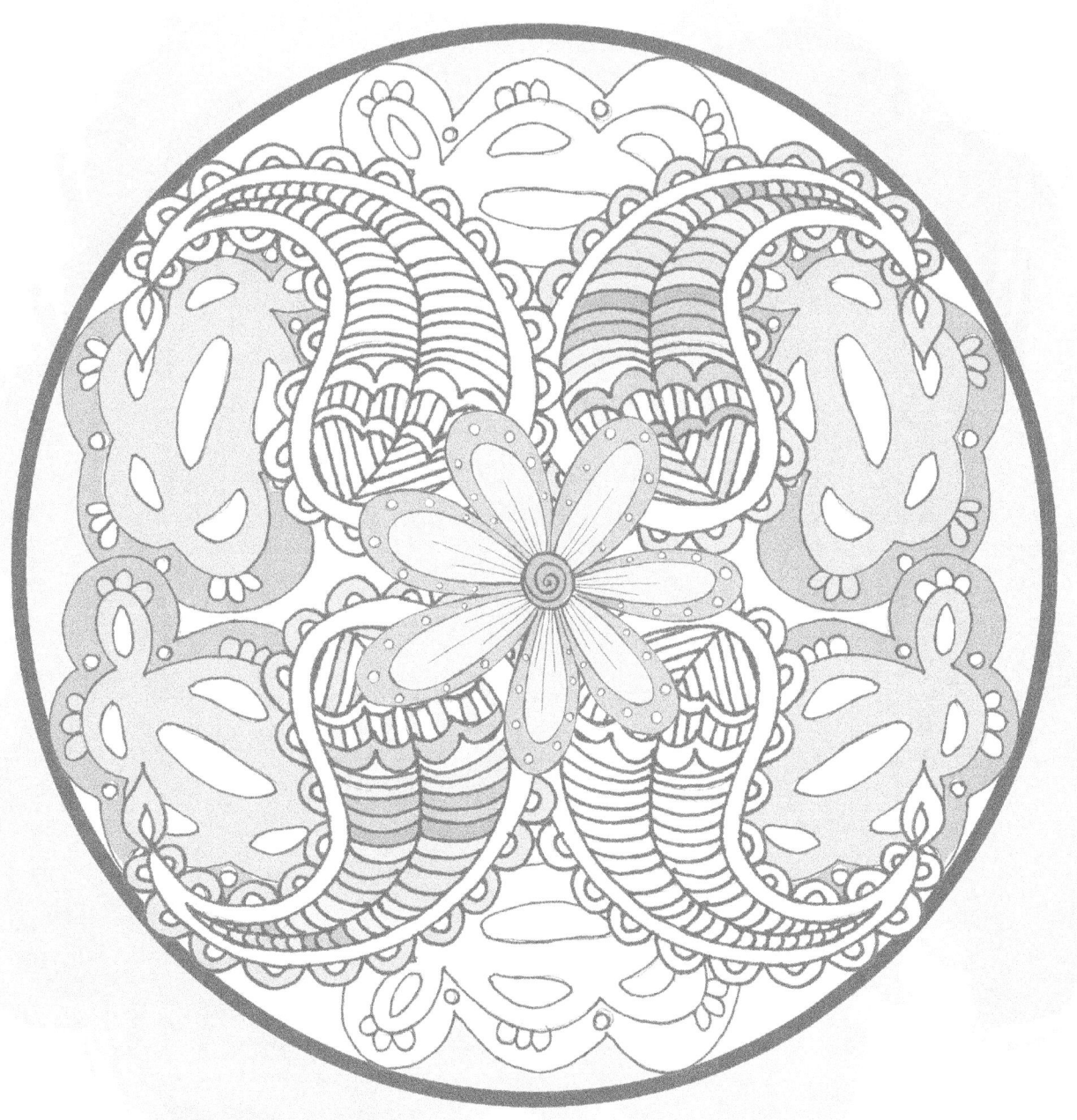

Edited by

# T.S. DOBSON

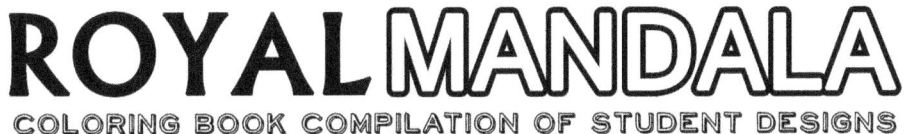

# ROYAL MANDALA
## COLORING BOOK COMPILATION OF STUDENT DESIGNS

Copyright 2016 by Jay High School

ISBN-13: 978-1523720781
ISBN-10: 1523720786

Cover Art by Instructor/Editor and Illustrator Teresa Scott Dobson

Back cover preview art created by students: Top Left—Kassadi Borders; Top Middle—Victor Mishoe; Top Right—Matthew Taylor; Bottom Left—Kayla Harrison; Bottom Middle—Brittany Ates; Bottom Right—Breanna Lambeth

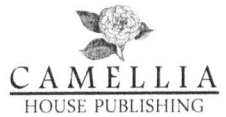

CAMELLIA
HOUSE PUBLISHING

Camellia House Publishing, Century, FL
**Printed in the United States of America.**

camelliahousepublishing@aol.com

# BEFORE YOU GET STARTED!

1. Put away all of the worldly distractions around you -- TV, phone, computer, etc.

2. Take out some color pencils, markers or crayons.

3. Pick a page and go with it. There's no particular order to follow.

4. When you finish a design, personalize it by signing your name anywhere on the page.

5. Stop when you need a break, then pick it up again later.

6. When finished, if you desire, share your creations with others!

7. Enjoy the extra blank sheets and do your own designs at the back of the book.

8. One more important tip… make sure to place a blank sheet of paper in between the page designs as you color to cut down on ink bleed.

ENJOY!

On behalf of the Jay High School Art Department we appreciate your purchase of our diverse collection of young artists' works. All proceeds go back to the Jay High School Art Department to help with the purchase of art supplies for our students.

We would love to see any of your finished creations! Send a picture of your art to *royalmandala@aol.com or visit us on Facebook and upload your art to Royal Mandala!*

*(Attach jpeg files 10 megs or less per email)*

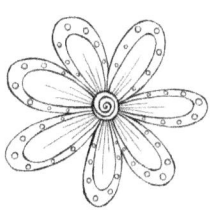

*"Your attitude is like a box of crayons that color your world. Constantly color your picture gray, and your picture will always be bleak. Try adding some bright colors to the picture by including humor, and your picture begins to lighten up."*

Allen Klein—Author and Pioneer in the study of laughter

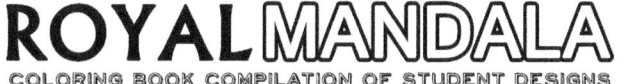

# ROYAL MANDALA
### COLORING BOOK COMPILATION OF STUDENT DESIGNS

## TABLE OF CONTENTS BY ARTIST:

1.  Teresa Dobson (Instructor)  /  11
2.  Aaron Campbell  /  13
3.  Alexis Mitchem  /  15
4.  Ally Settle  /  17
5.  Alyssa Baxley  /  19
6.  Alyssa Tranter  /  21
7.  Austin Gonzalez  /  23
8.  Autumn Ates  /  25
9.  Bonnie Lambeth  /  27
10. Brandon Moye  /  29
11. Brandon White  /  31
12. Breanna Lambeth  /  33
13. Bridget Gibbs  /  35
14. Bristin Campbell  /  37
15. Brittany Ates  /  39
16. Brooklynne Wolters  /  41
17. Cameron Beasley  /  43
18. Cameron Driscoll  /  45
19. Carly Sanders  /  47
20. Casey Holley-Bray  /  49
21. Charliene Martin  /  51
22. Cori Ritter  /  53
23. Daniel Goforth  /  55
24. Devin Ashby  /  57
25. Dylan Crawford  /  59
26. Garrett Wolfe  /  61
27. Hannah Vaughn  /  63
28. James Eddings  /  65
29. Jamie Blackmon  /  67
30. Jorja Agrait  /  69

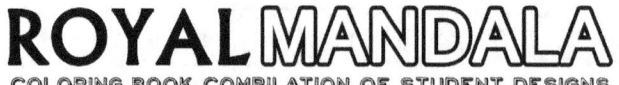

# ROYAL MANDALA
COLORING BOOK COMPILATION OF STUDENT DESIGNS

## TABLE OF CONTENTS BY ARTIST (CONTINUED) :

31. Joshua Barlow / 71

32. Justin NeSmith / 73

33. Kassadi Borders / 75

34. Katie Morton / 77

35. Kayla Harrison / 79

36. Kennedy Cato / 81

37. Layla Baldwin / 83

38. Luke Burkhead / 85

39. Maci Holt / 87

40. Madison McCurdy / 89

41. Makayla Thompson / 91

42. Matthew Boutwell / 93

43. Matthew Taylor / 95

44. Meghan Mayo / 97

45. Mia Granberry / 99

46. Morgan Floyd / 101

47. Nathan Dunsford / 103

48. Nathan Stanford / 105

49. Olivia Cook / 107

50. Olivia Fornwalt / 109

51. Pamela Fornwalt / 111

52. Regan Strength / 113

53. Samantha Fupler / 115

54. Sarah Geck / 117

55. Shelby Edwards / 119

56. Shelby Moore / 121

57. Tatum Porter / 123

58. Taylor Scott / 125

59. Tyler Blackmon / 127

60. Victor Mishoe / 129

*DRAWING PAD* / 131

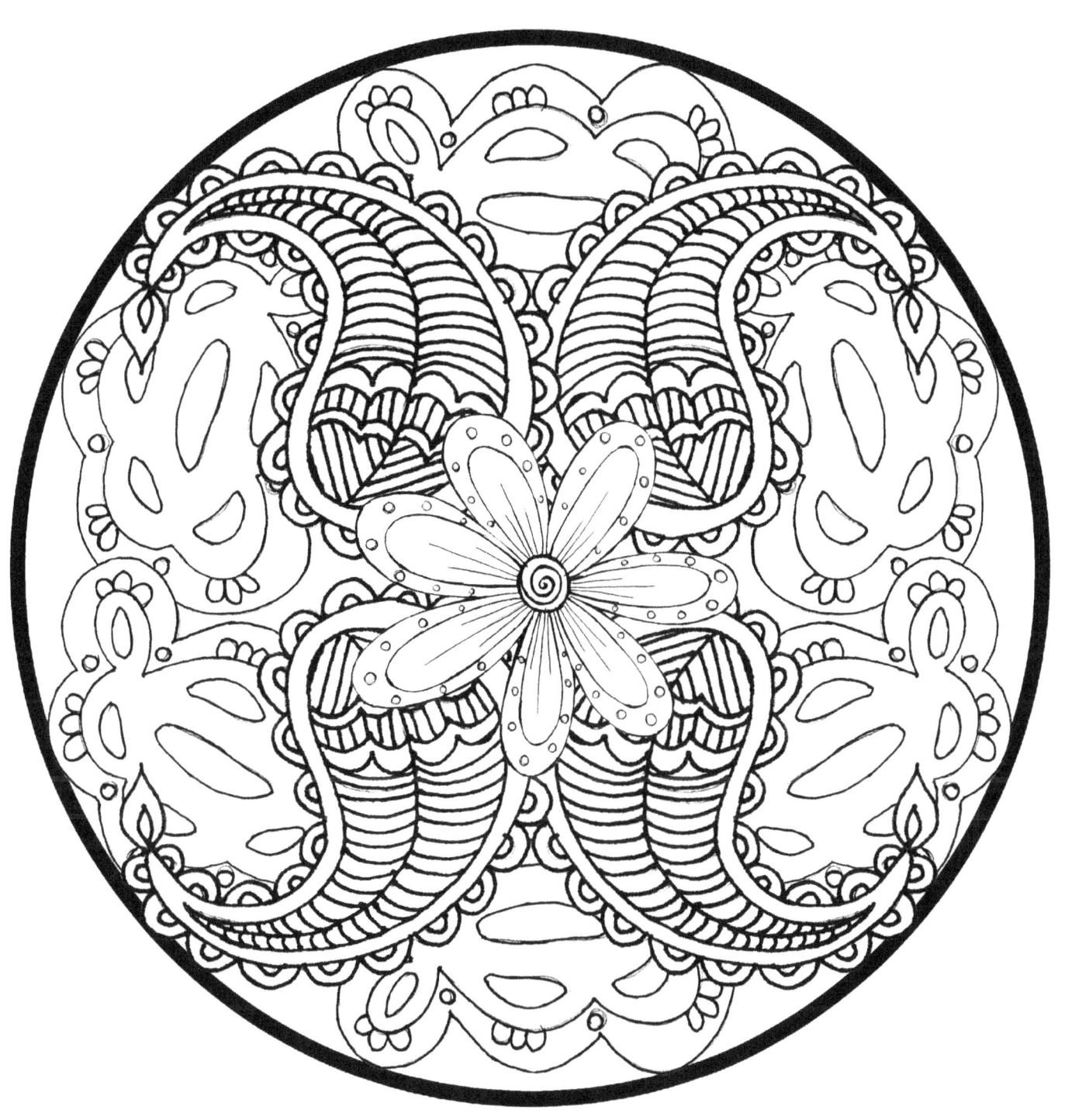

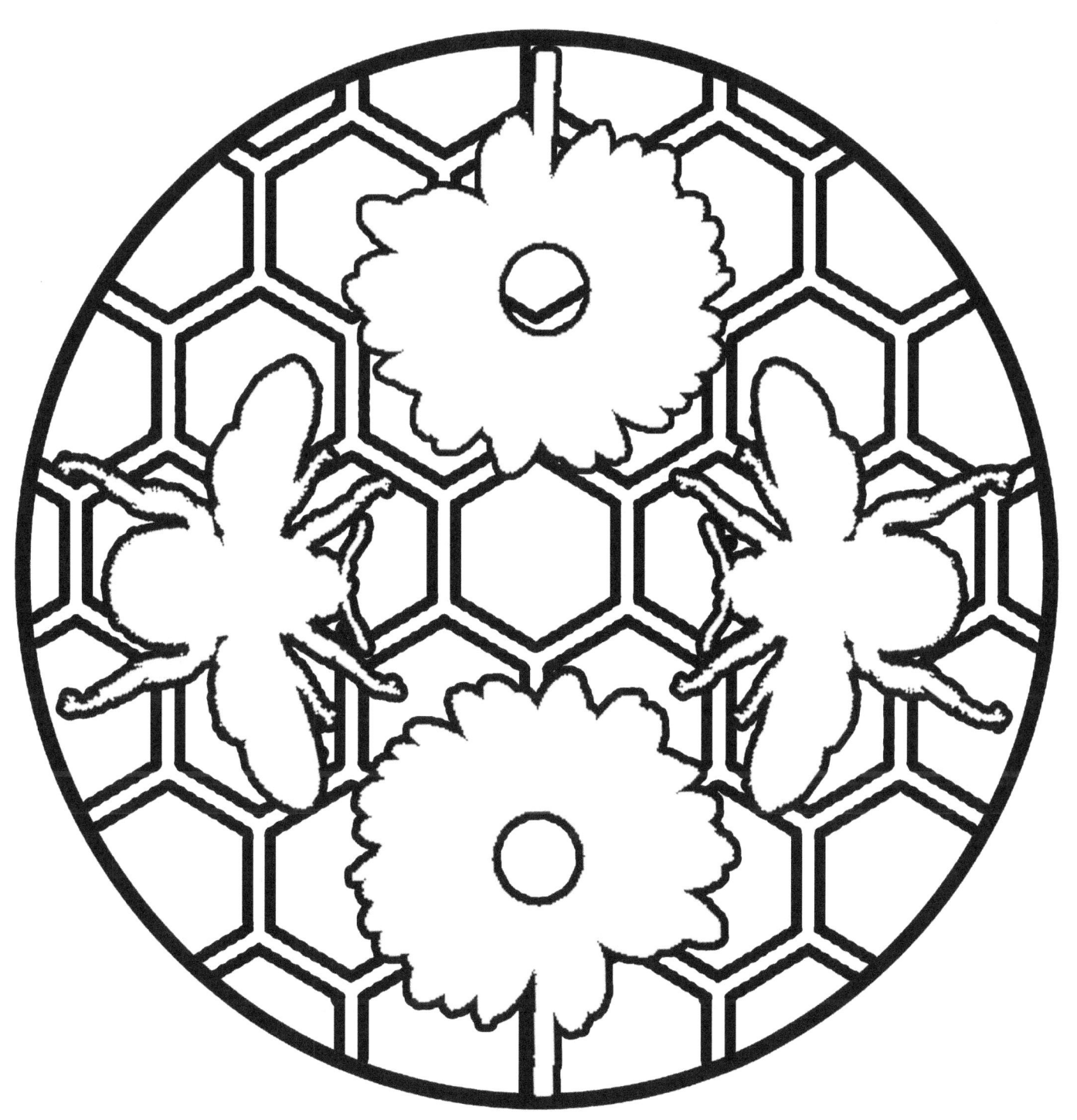

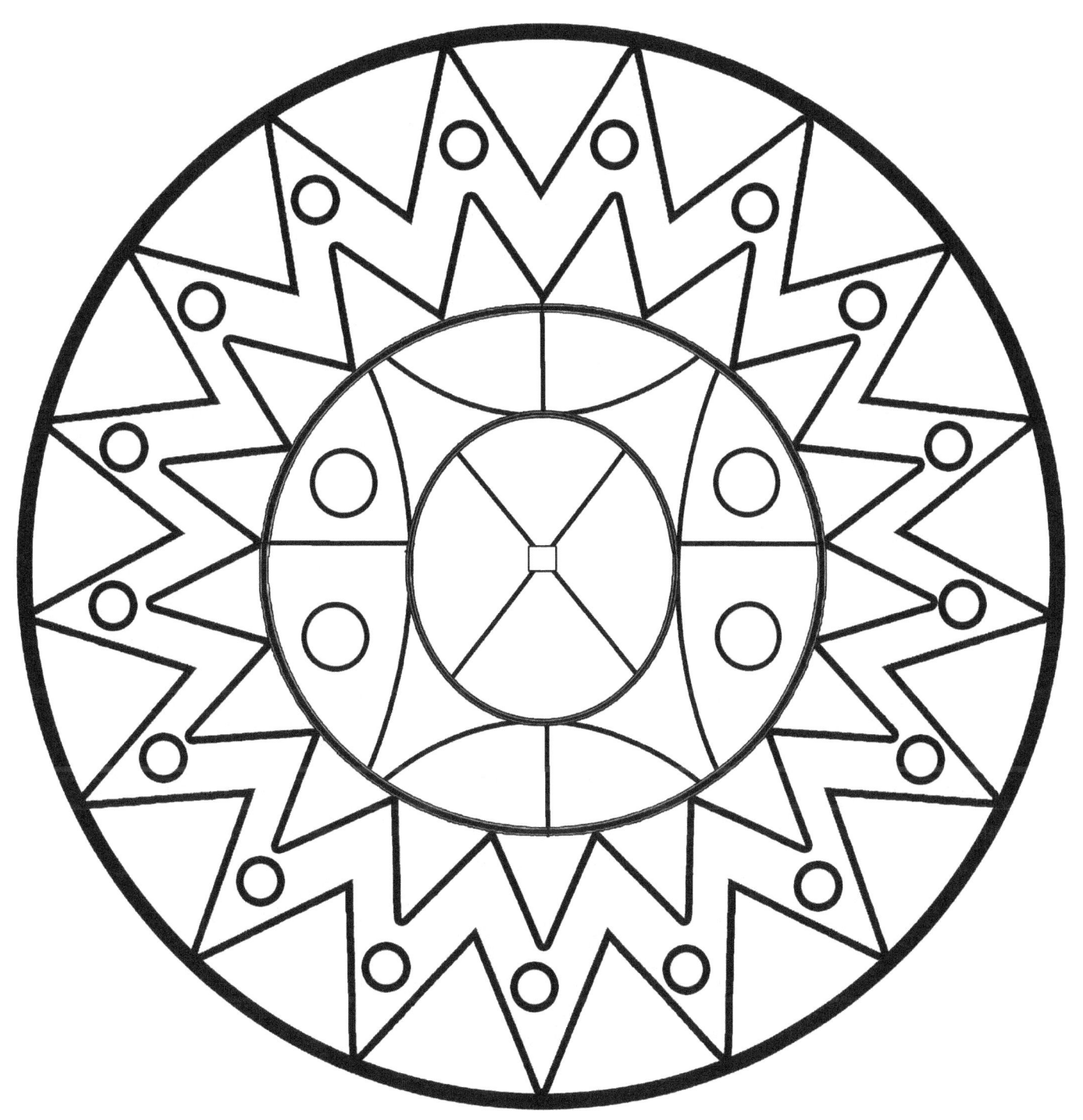

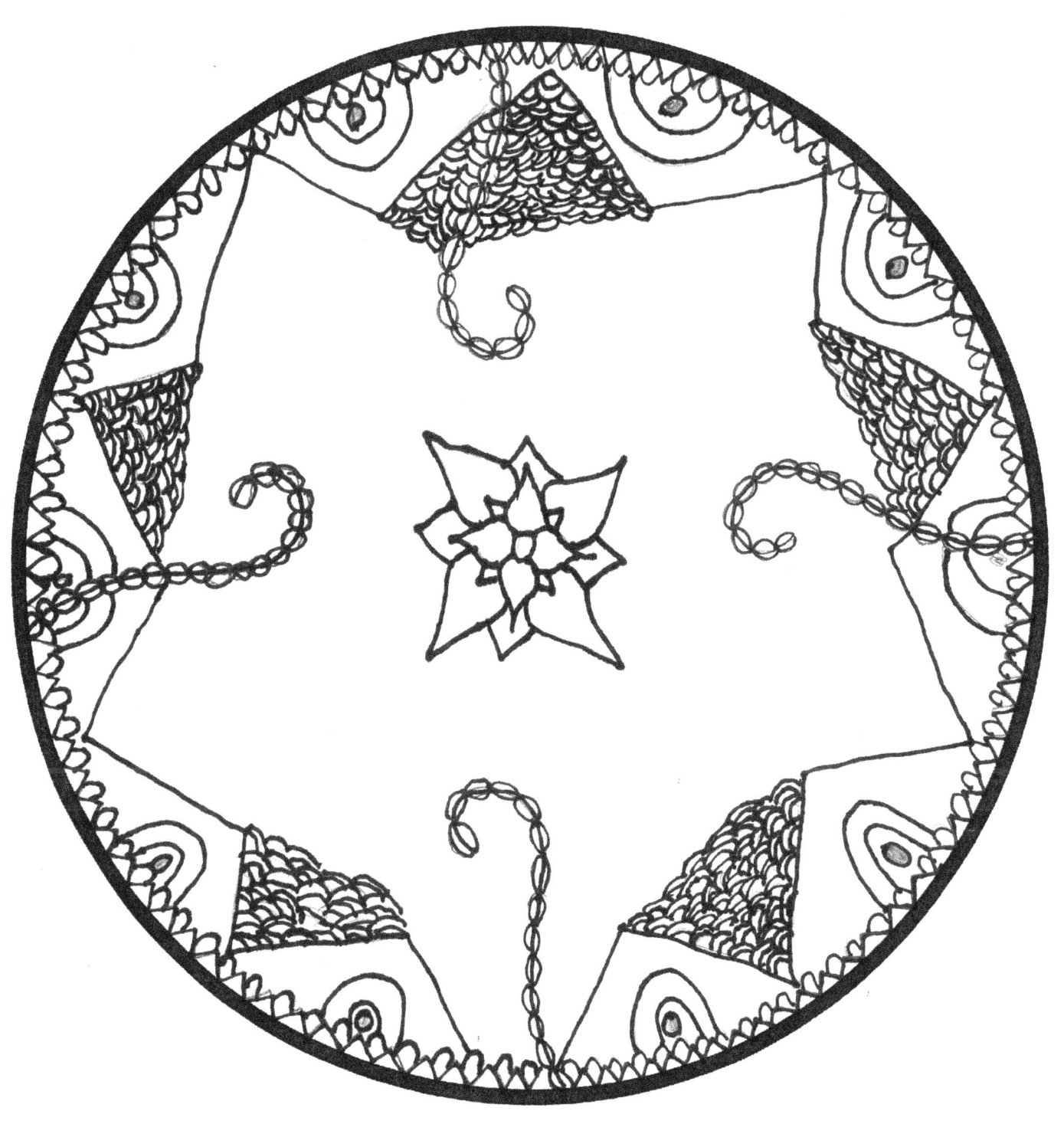

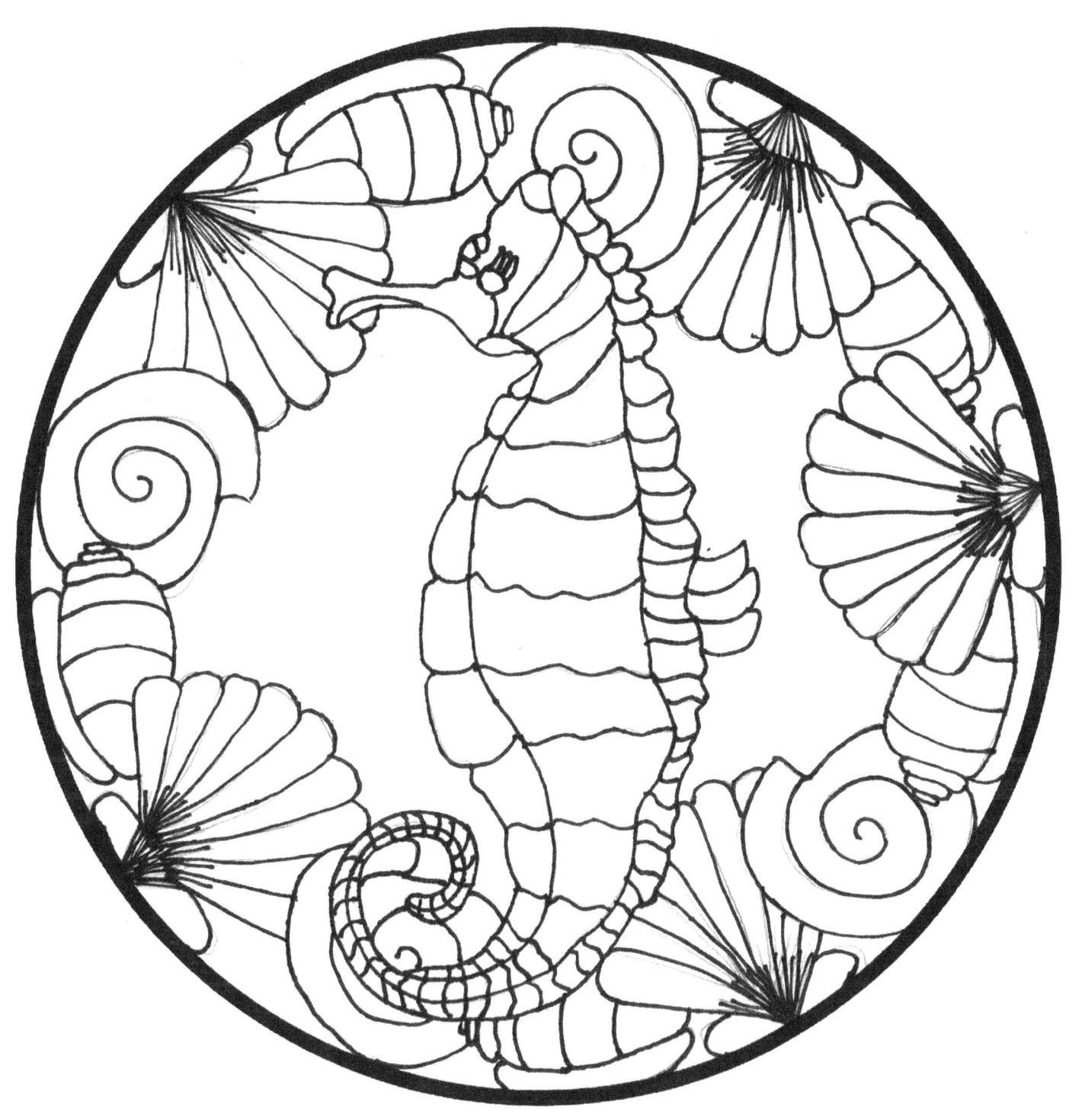

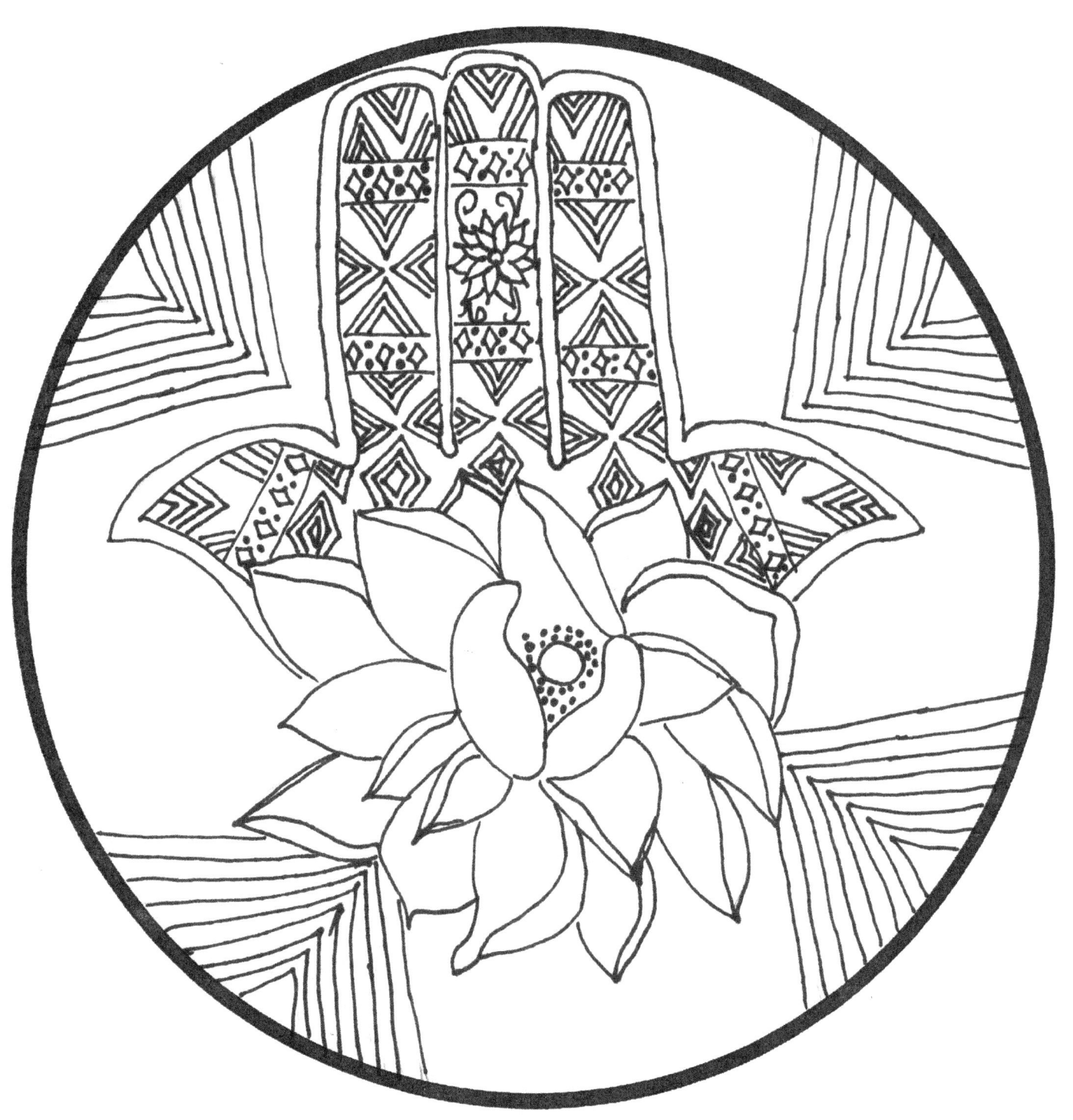

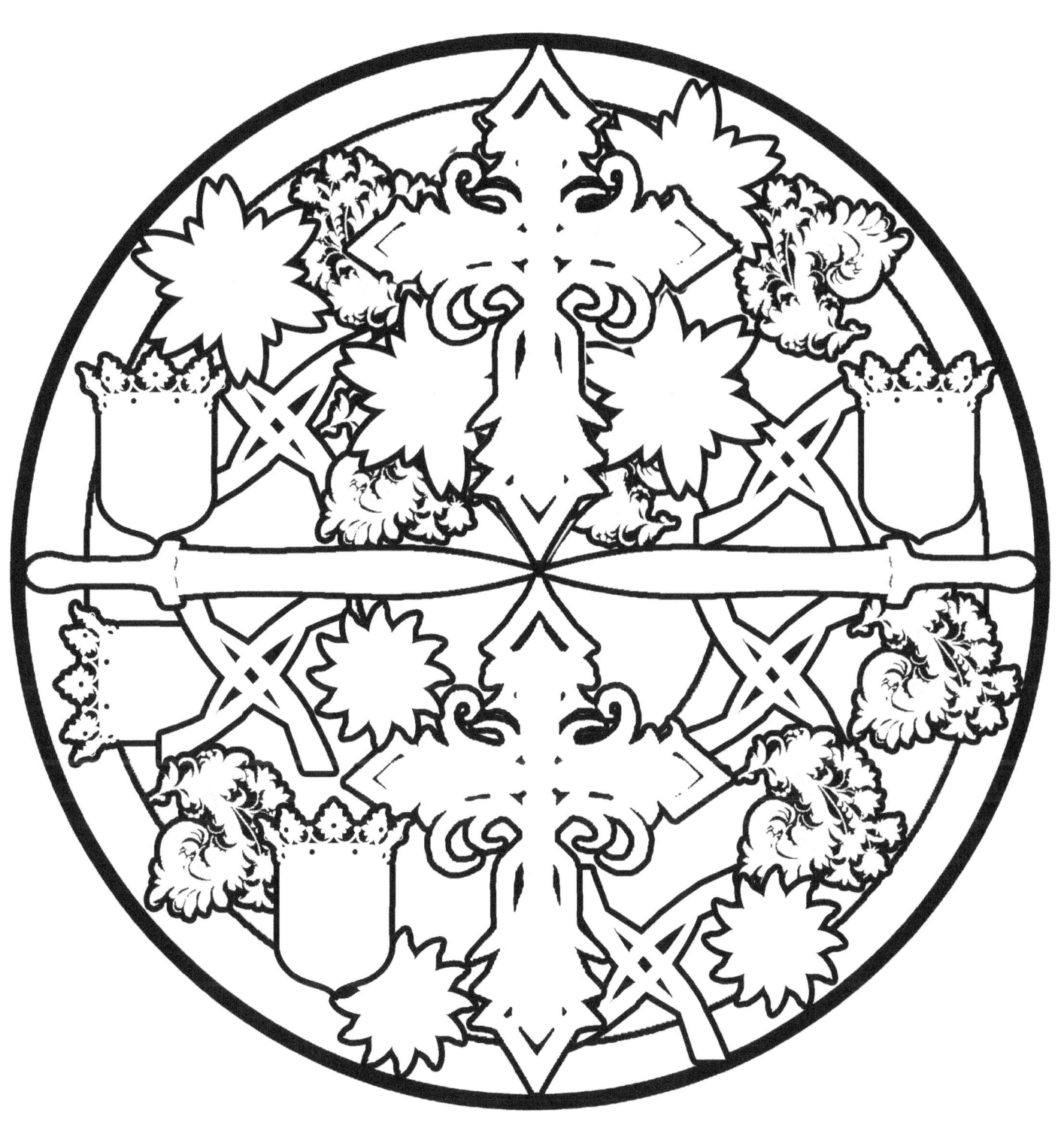

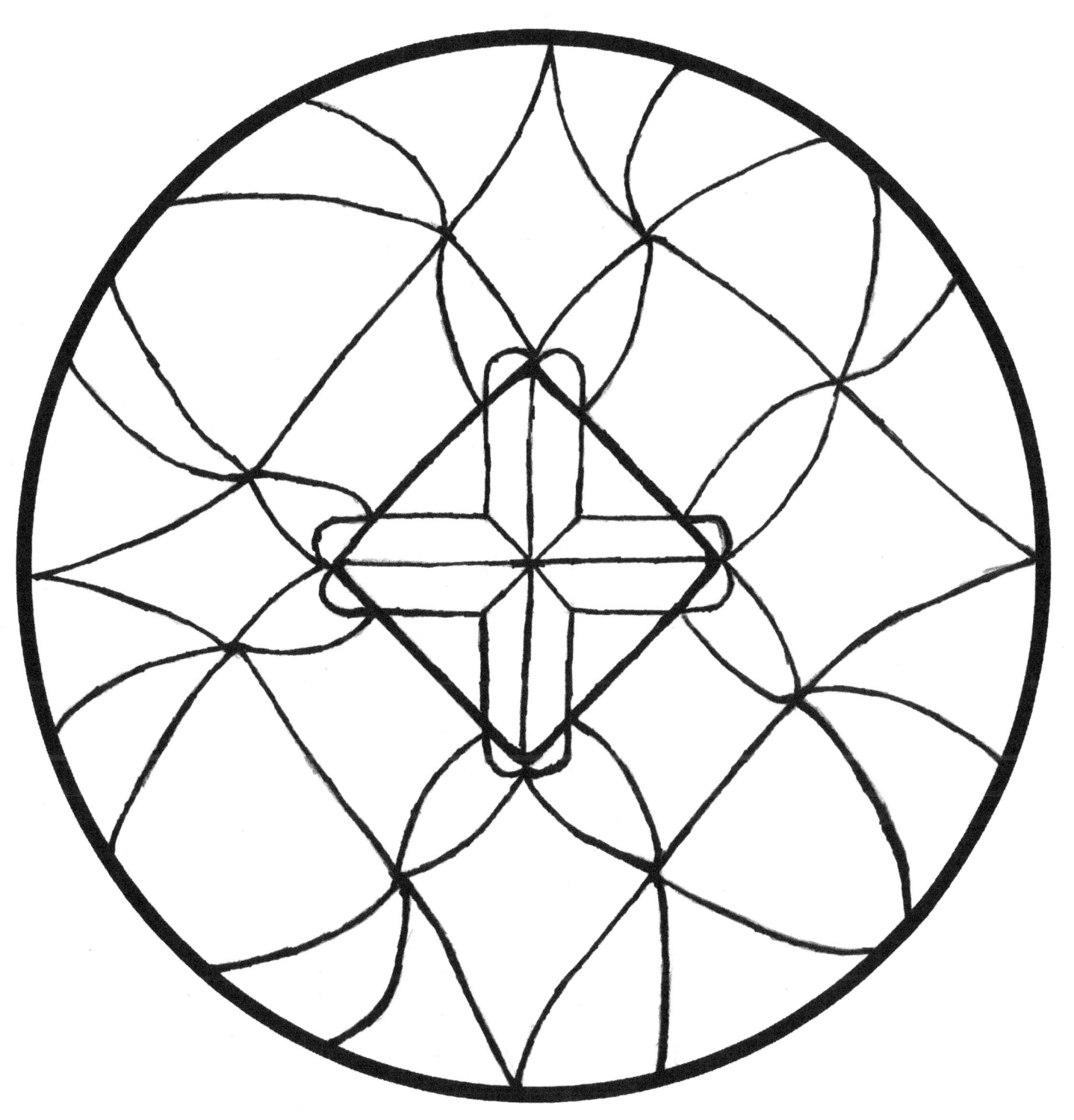

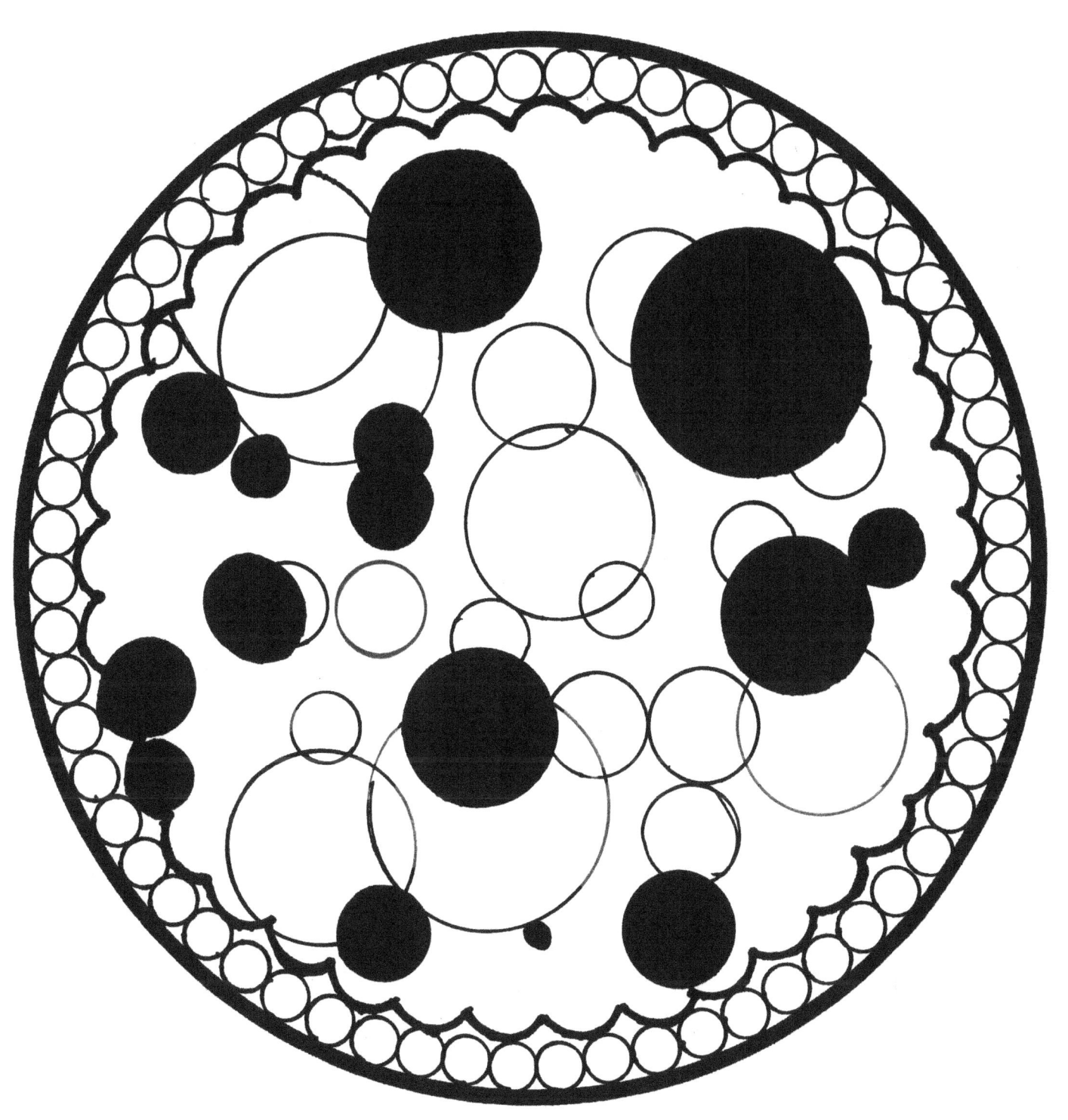

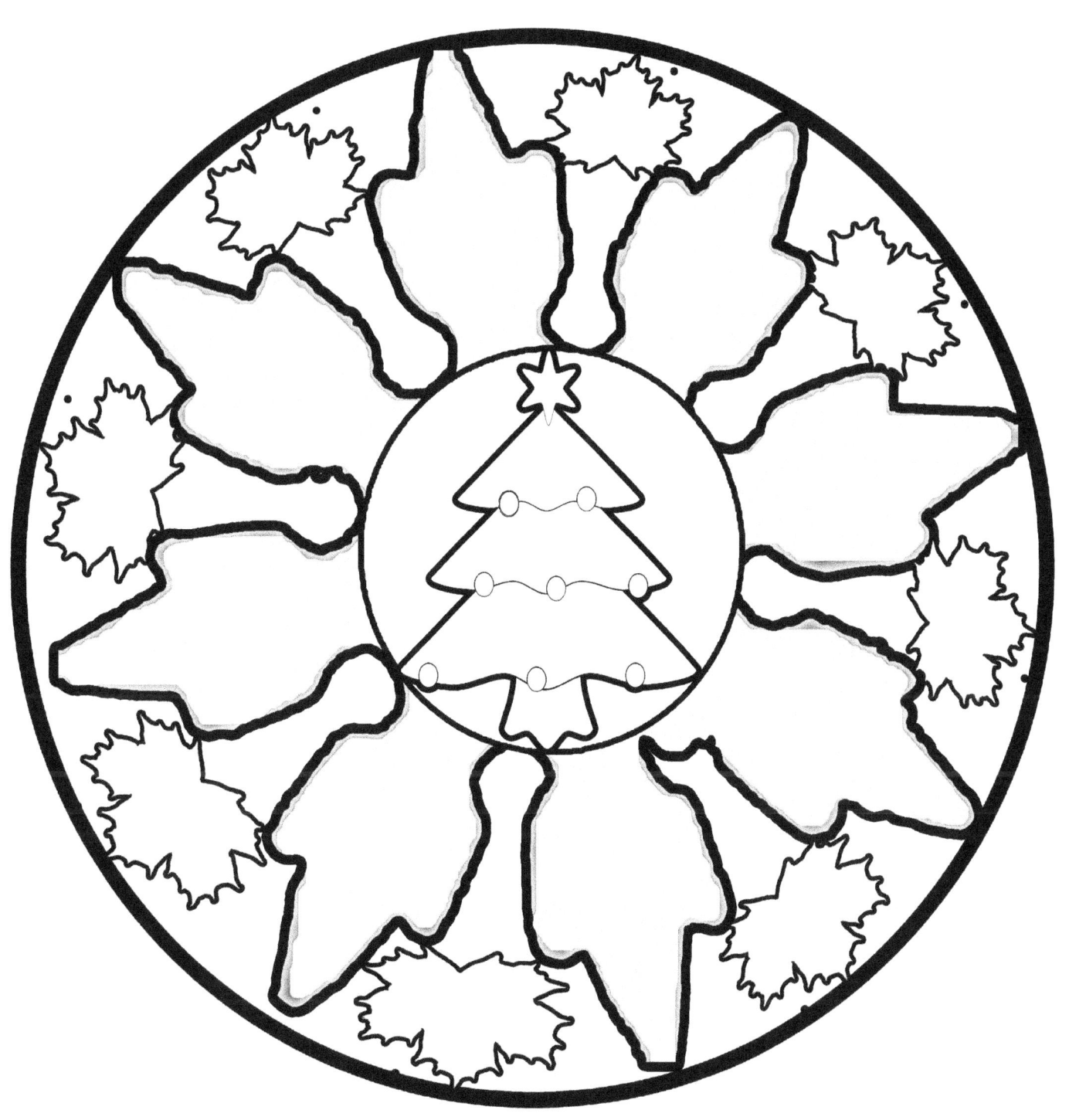

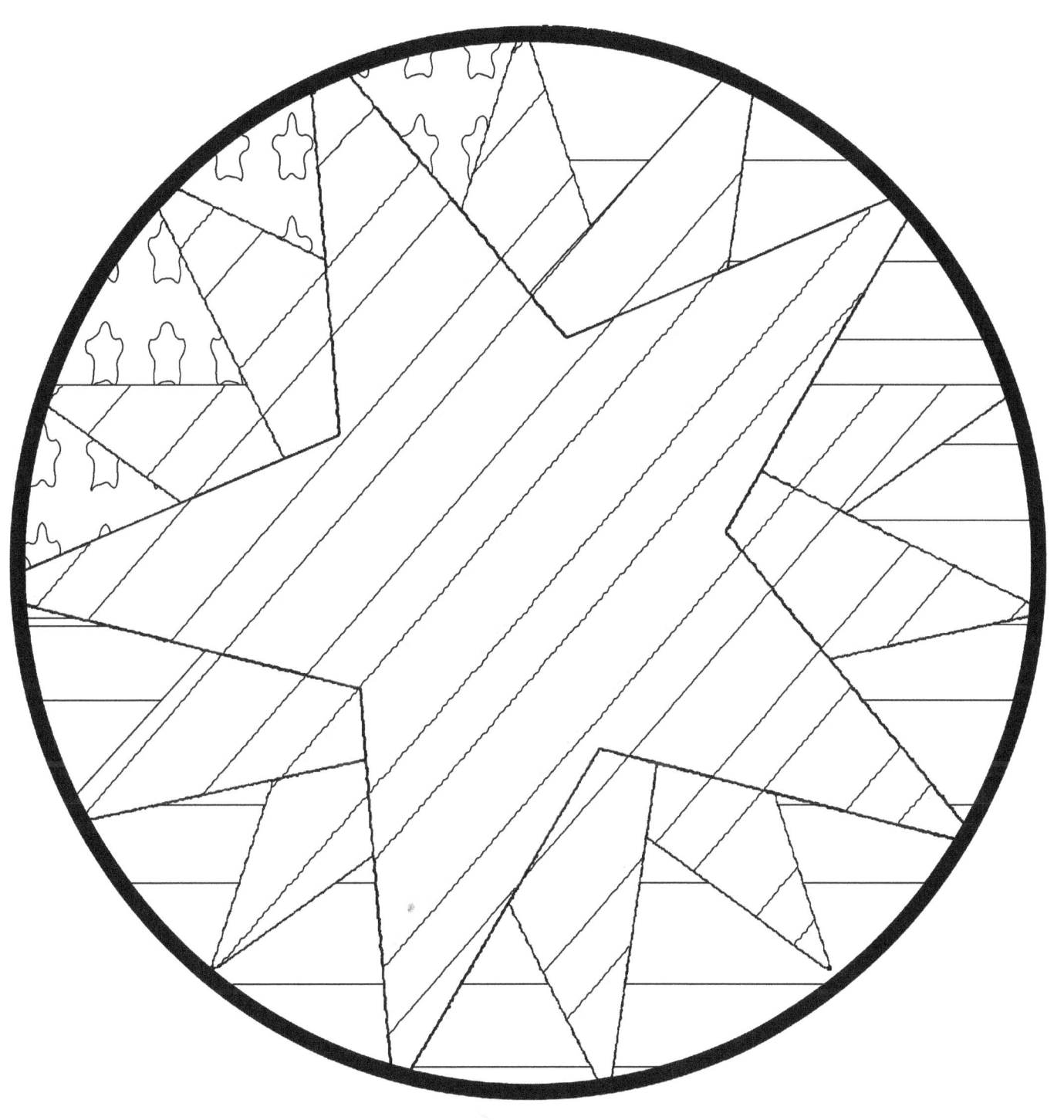

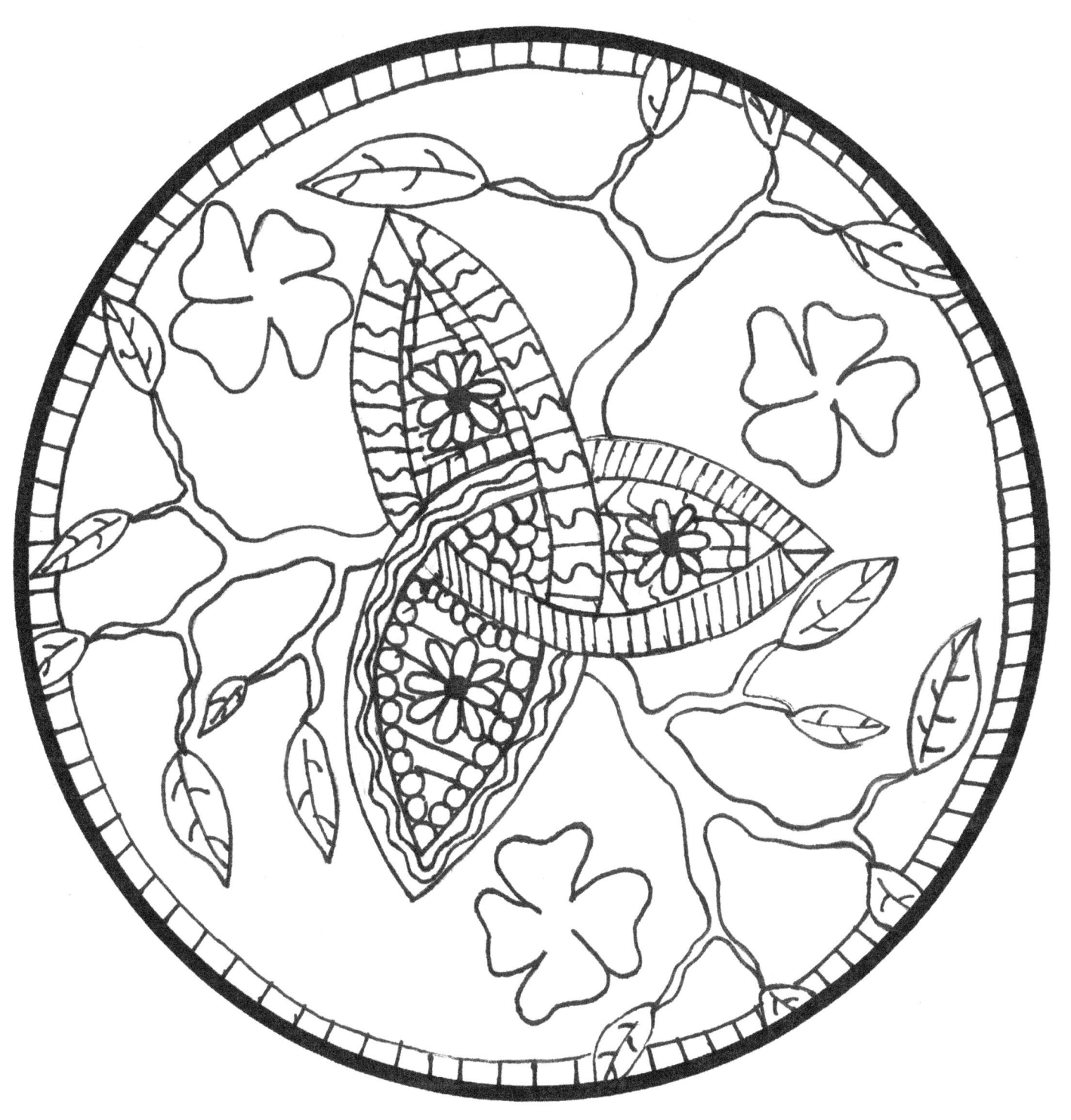

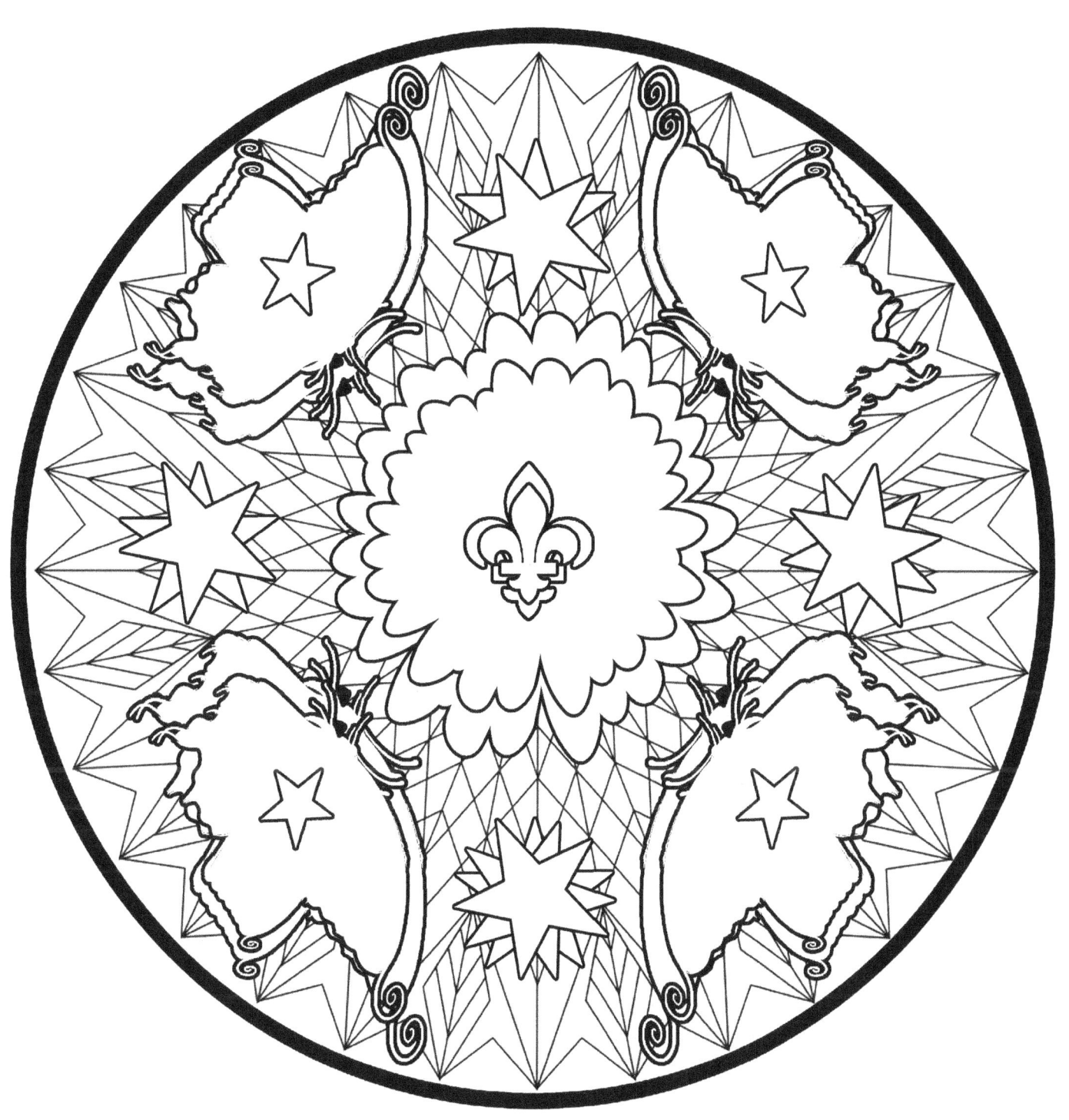

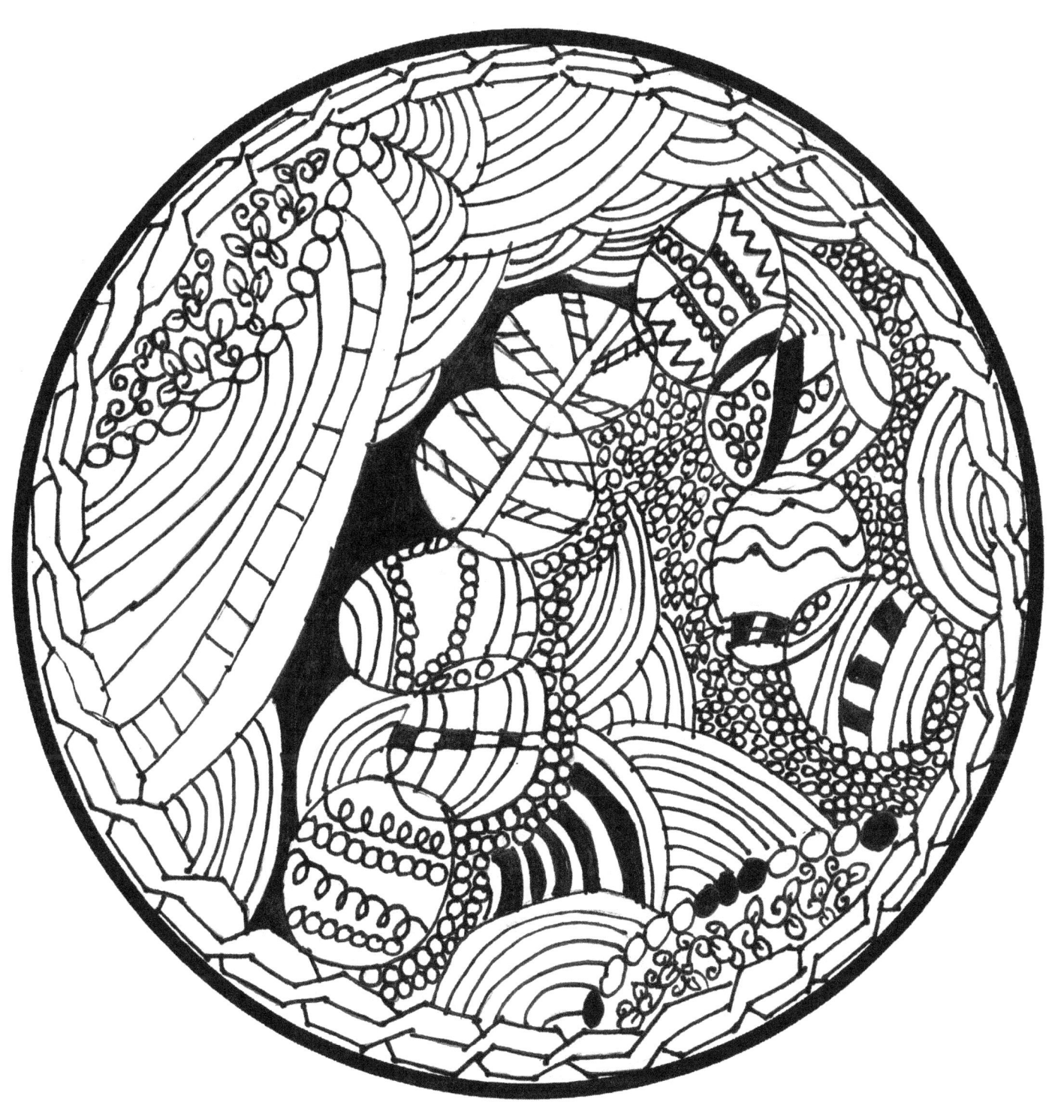

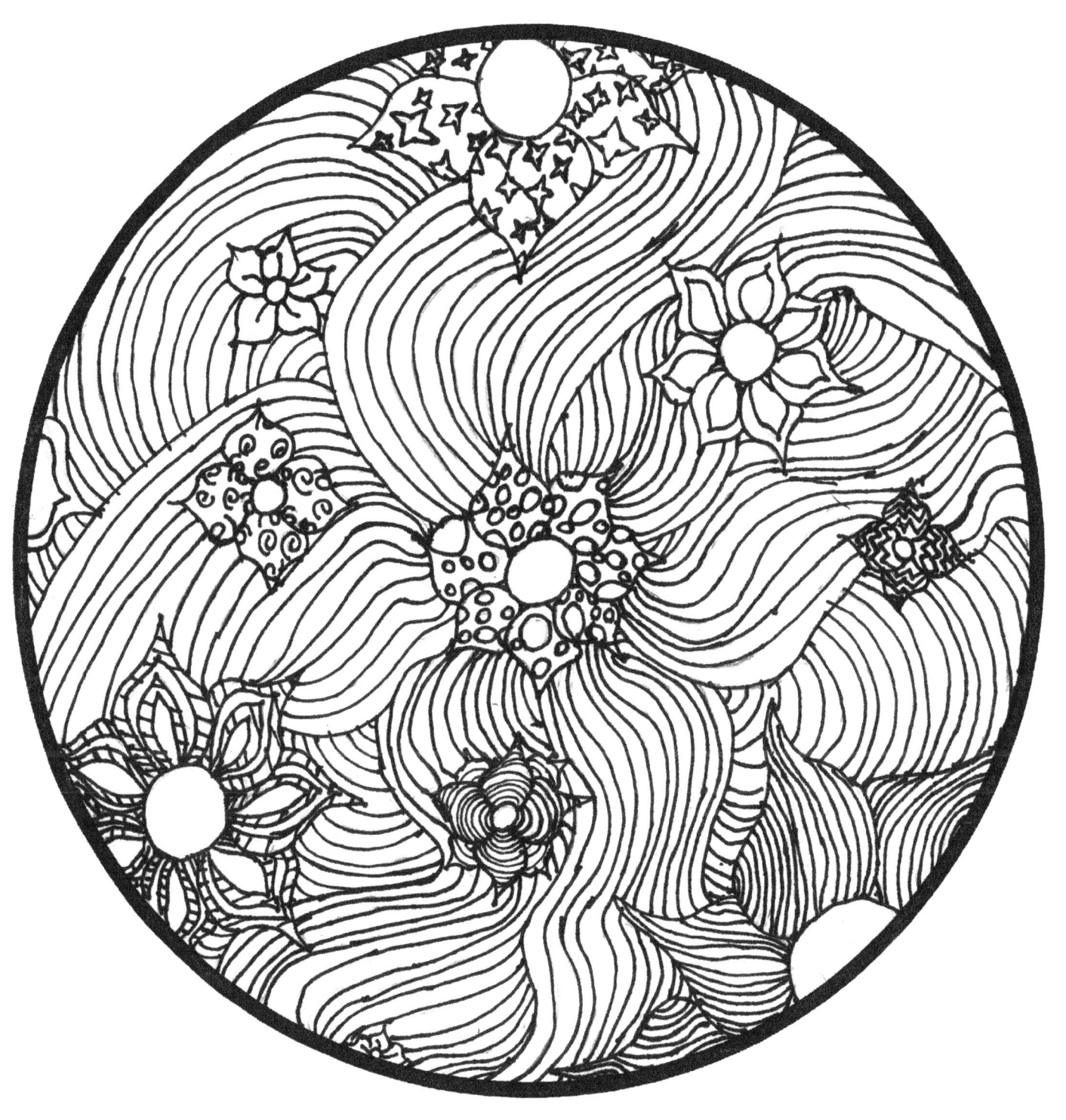

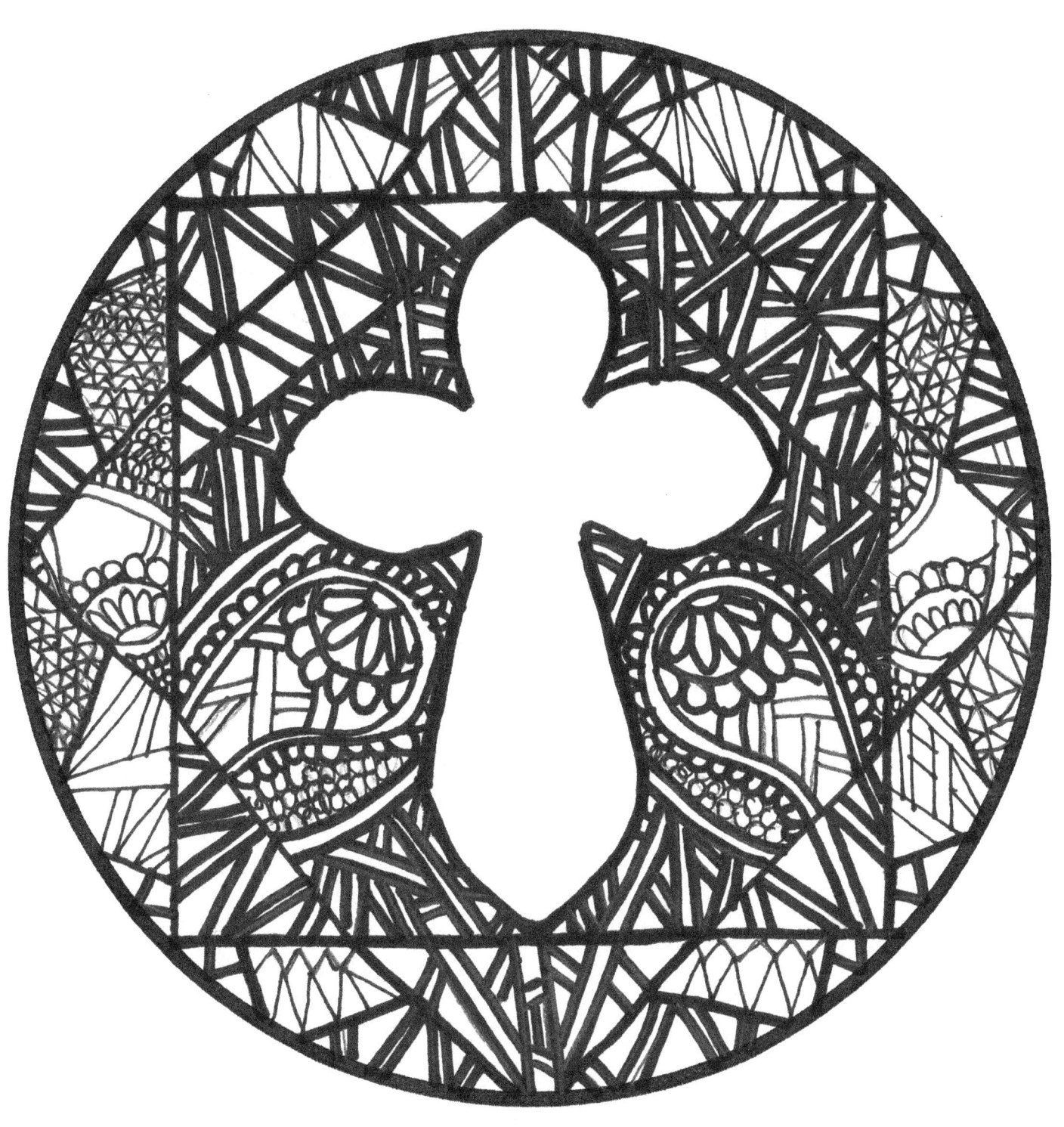

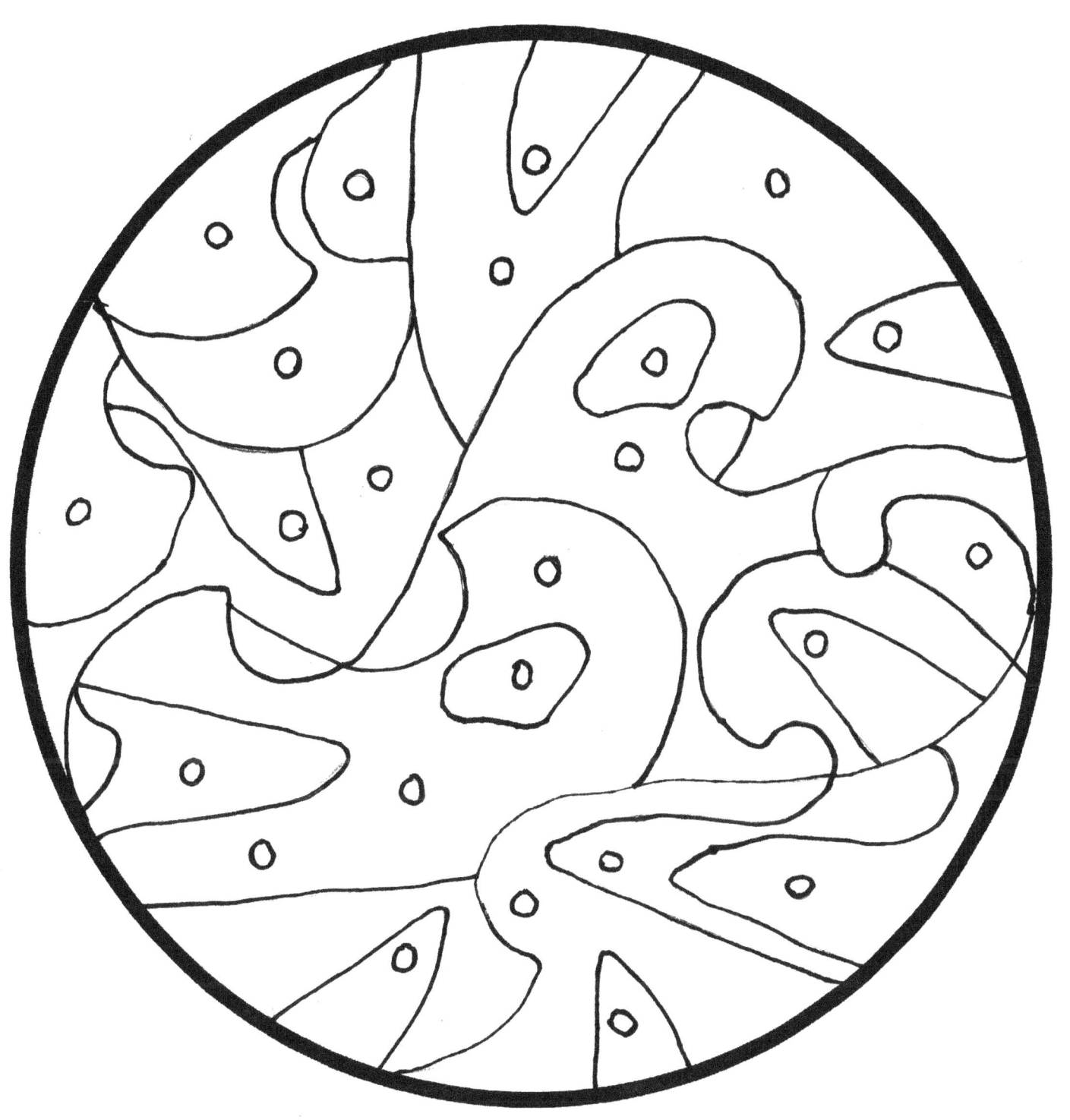

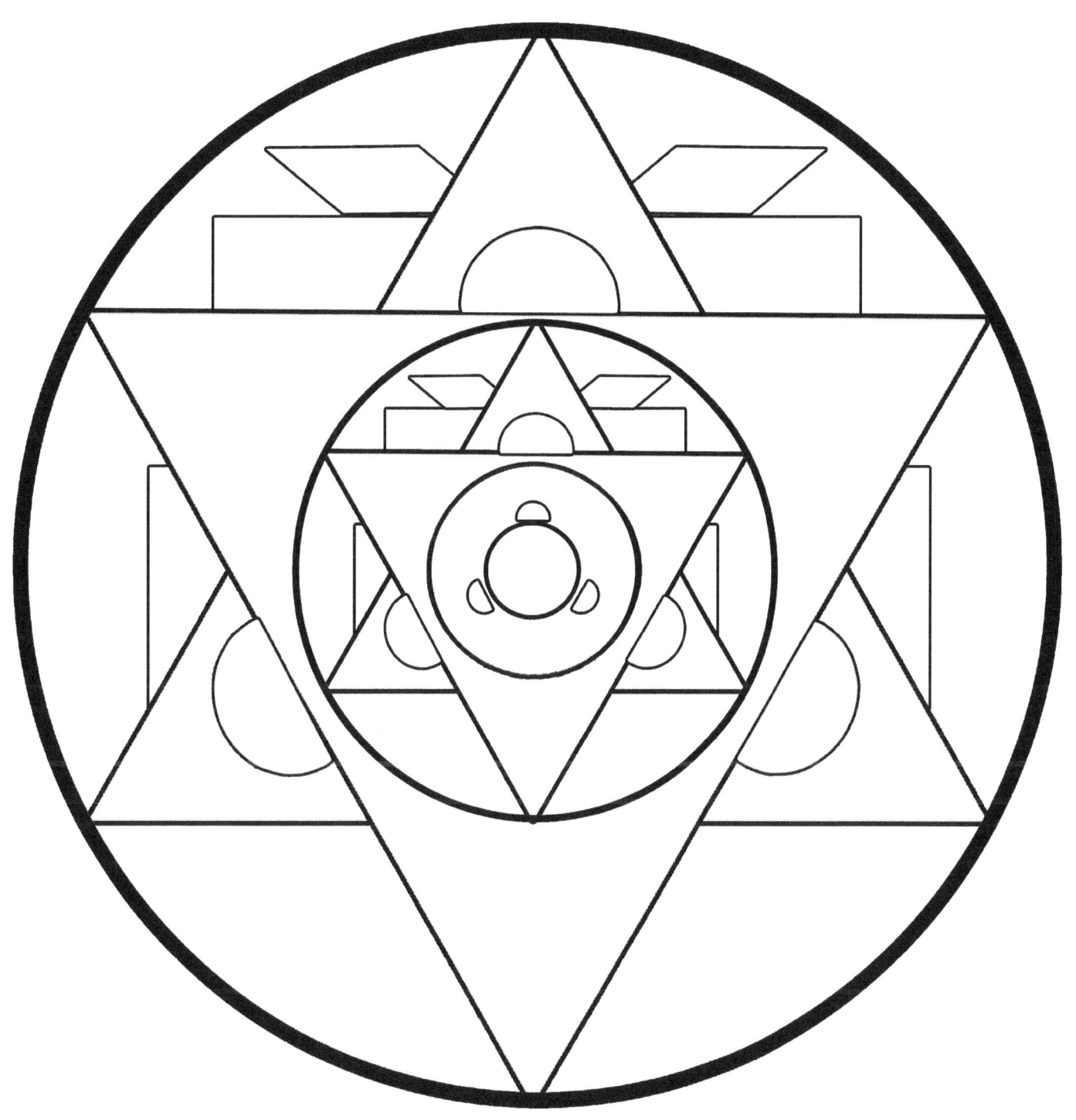

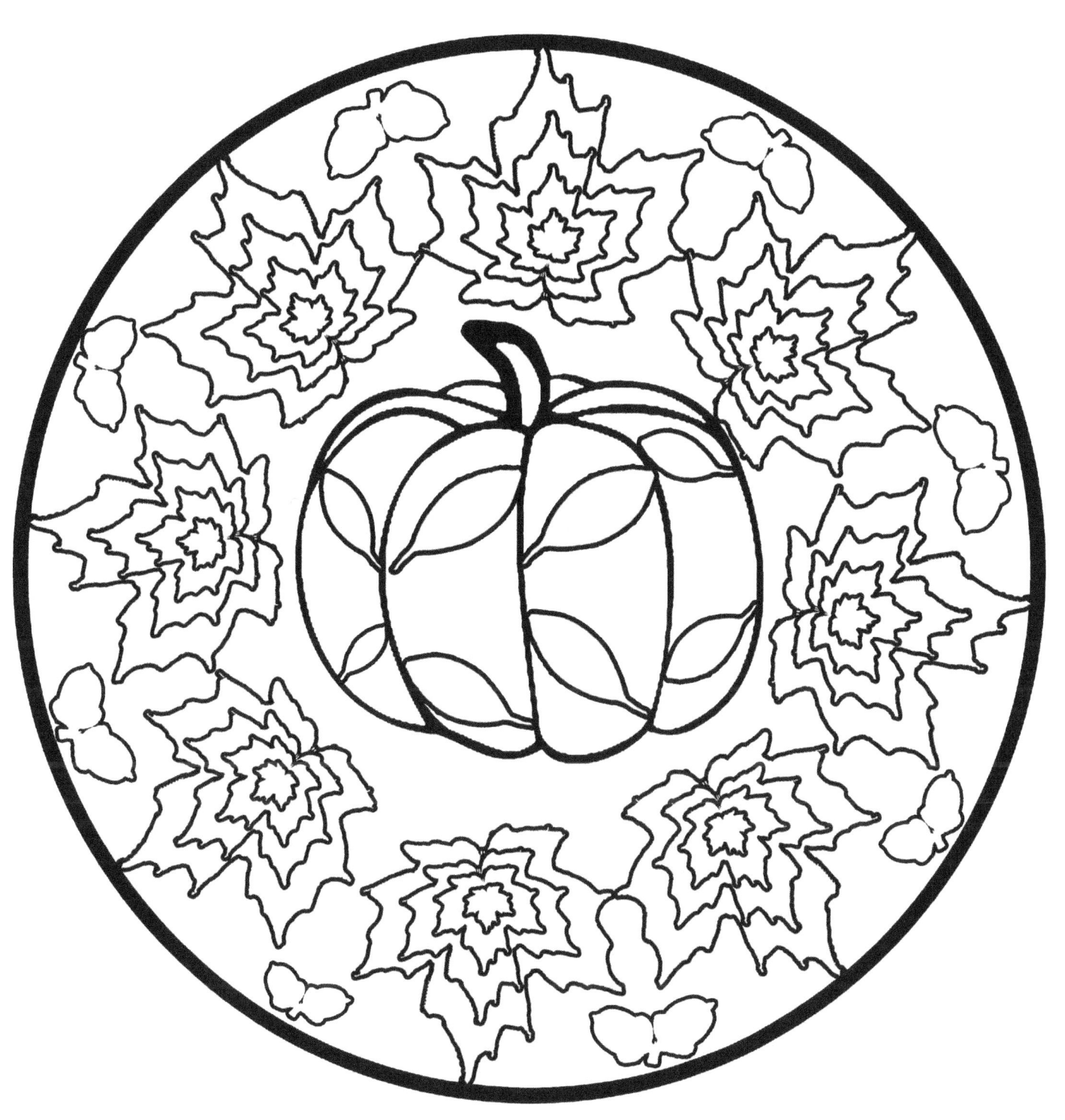

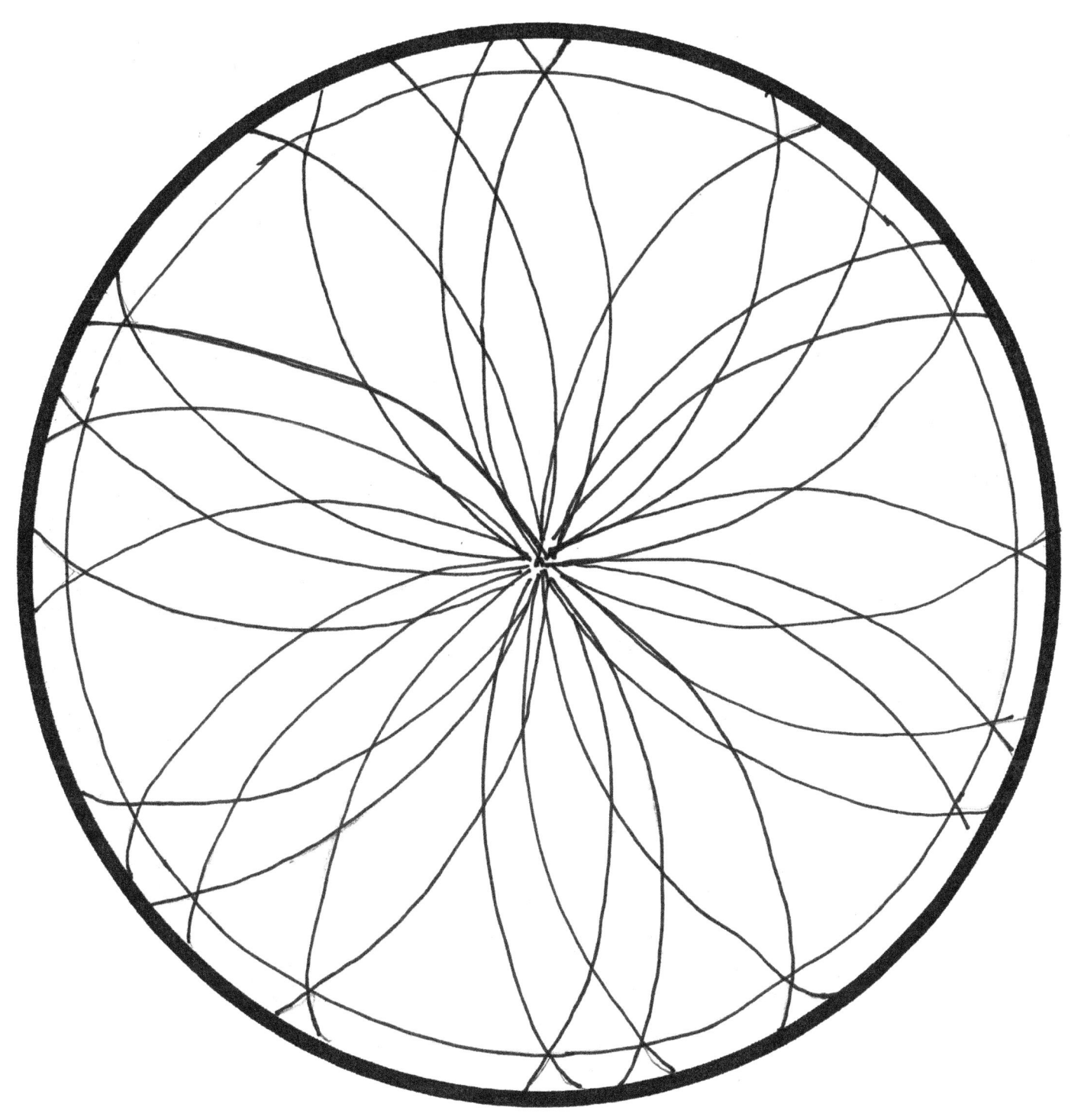

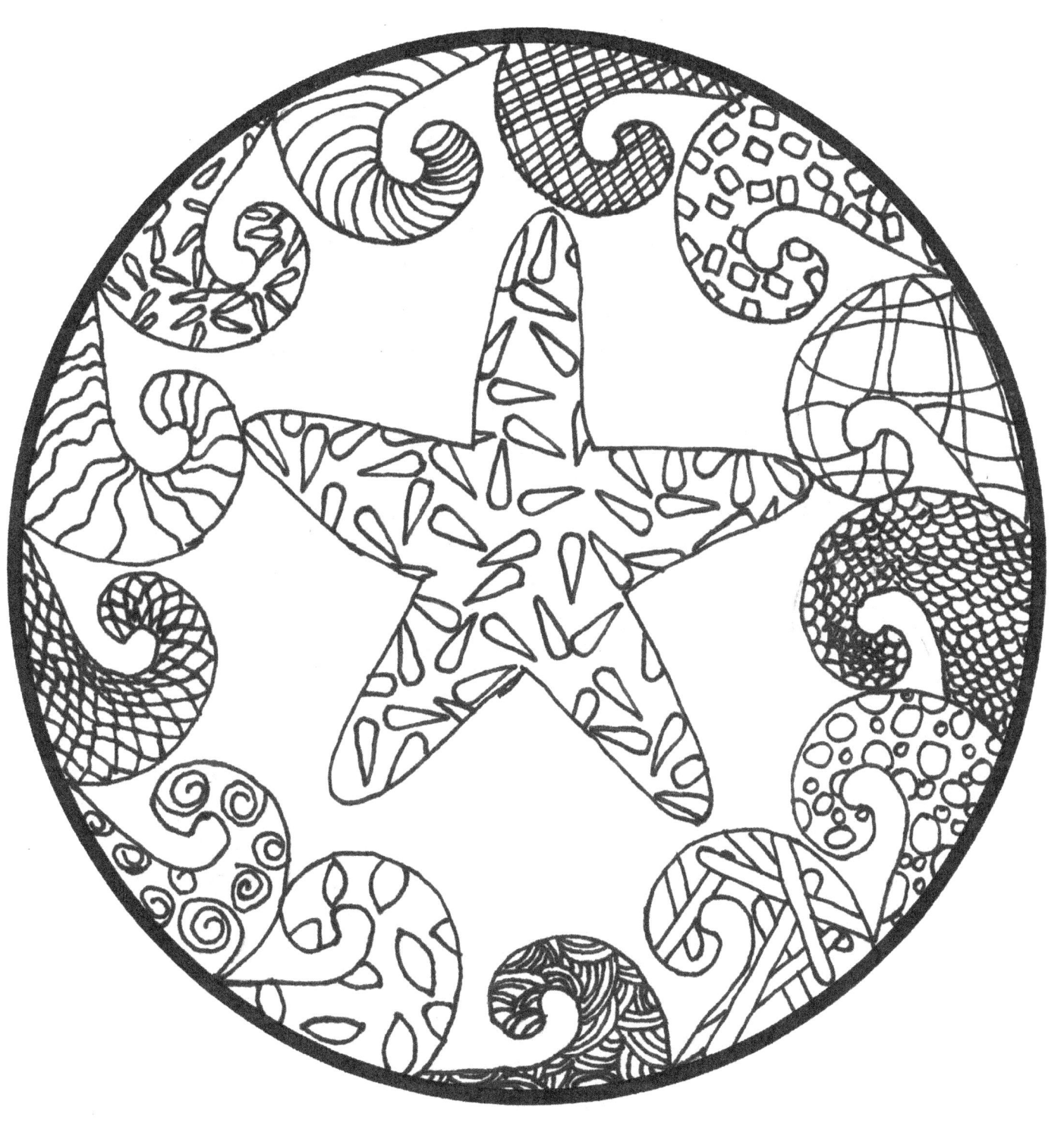

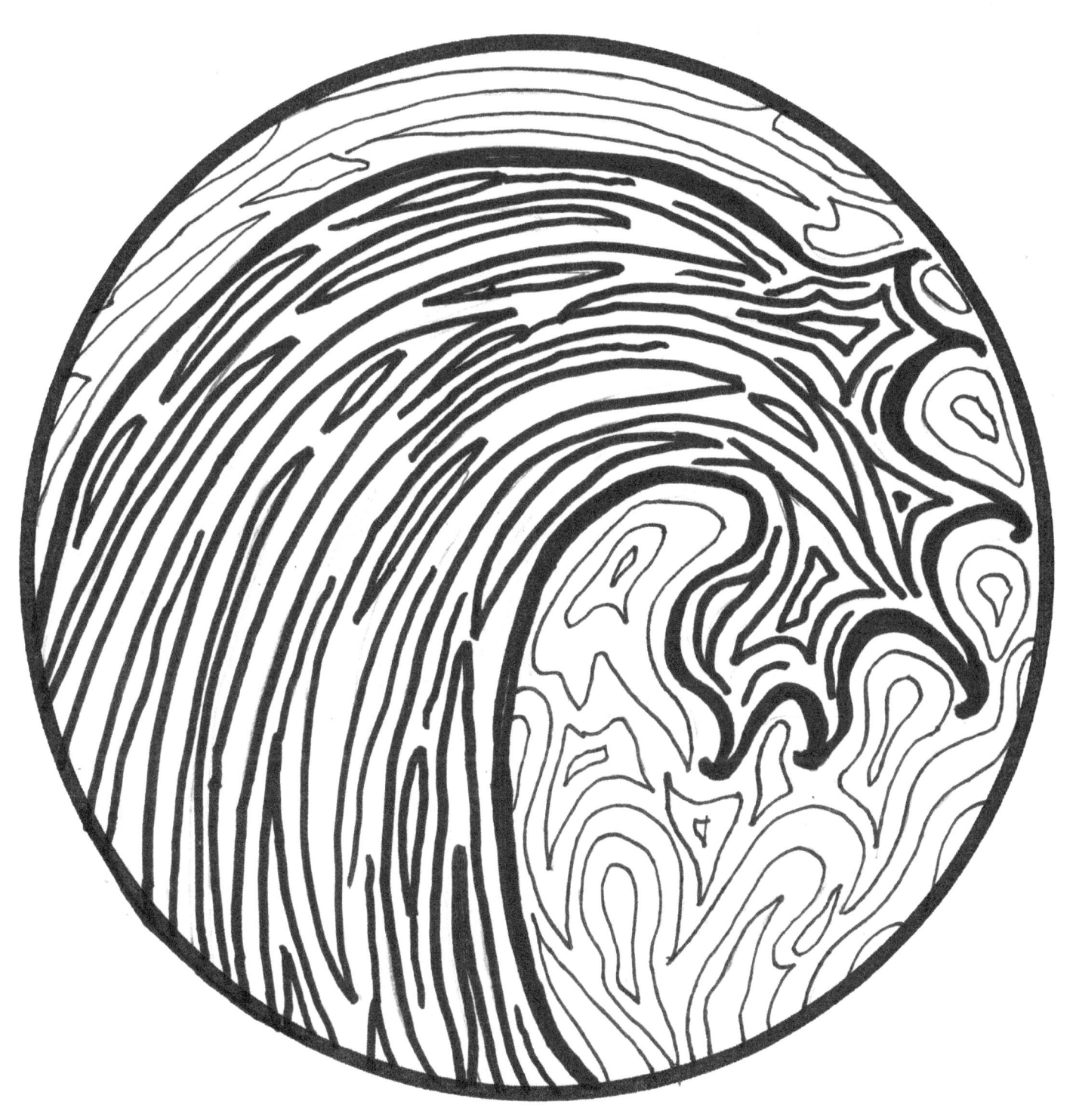

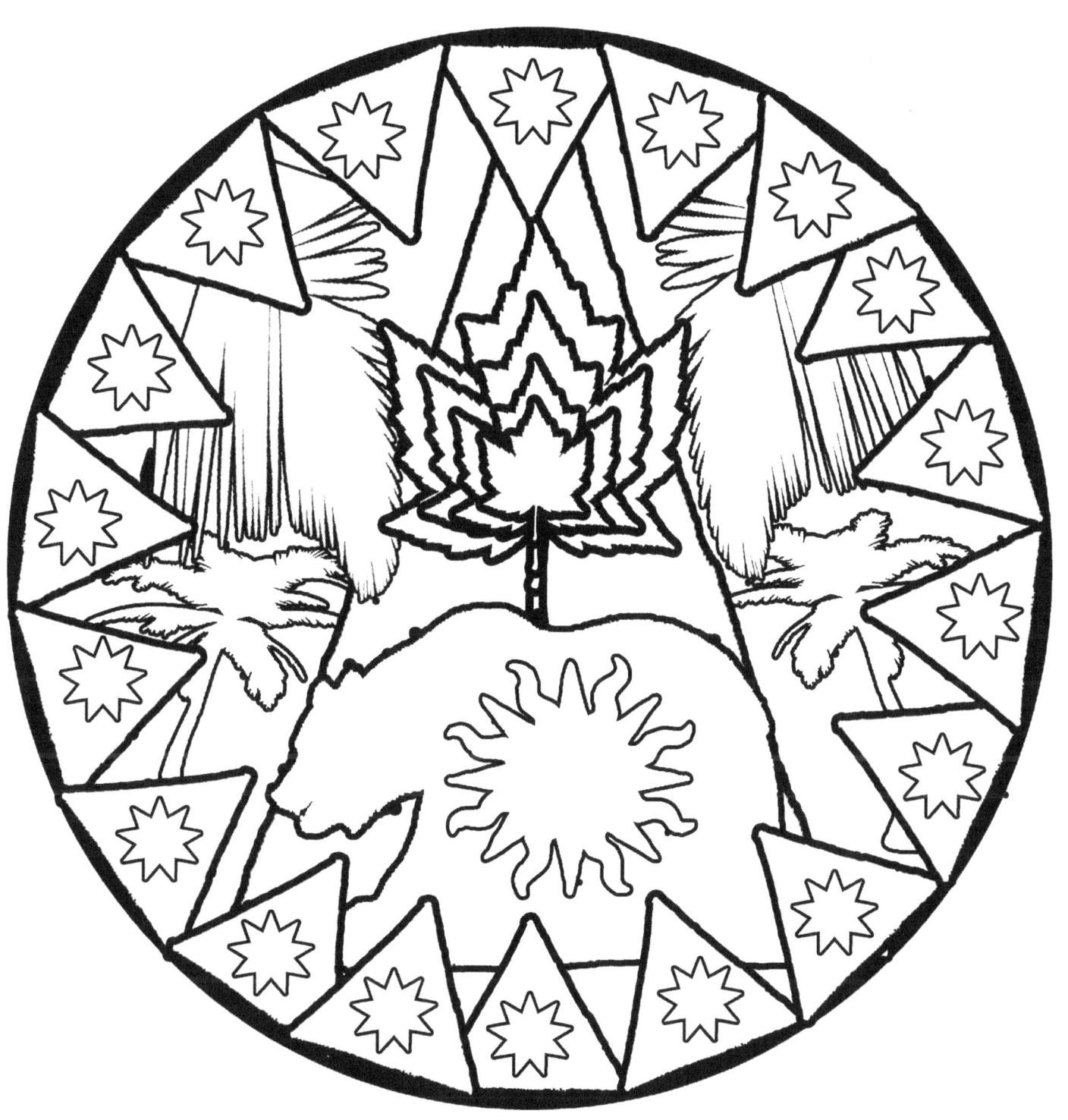

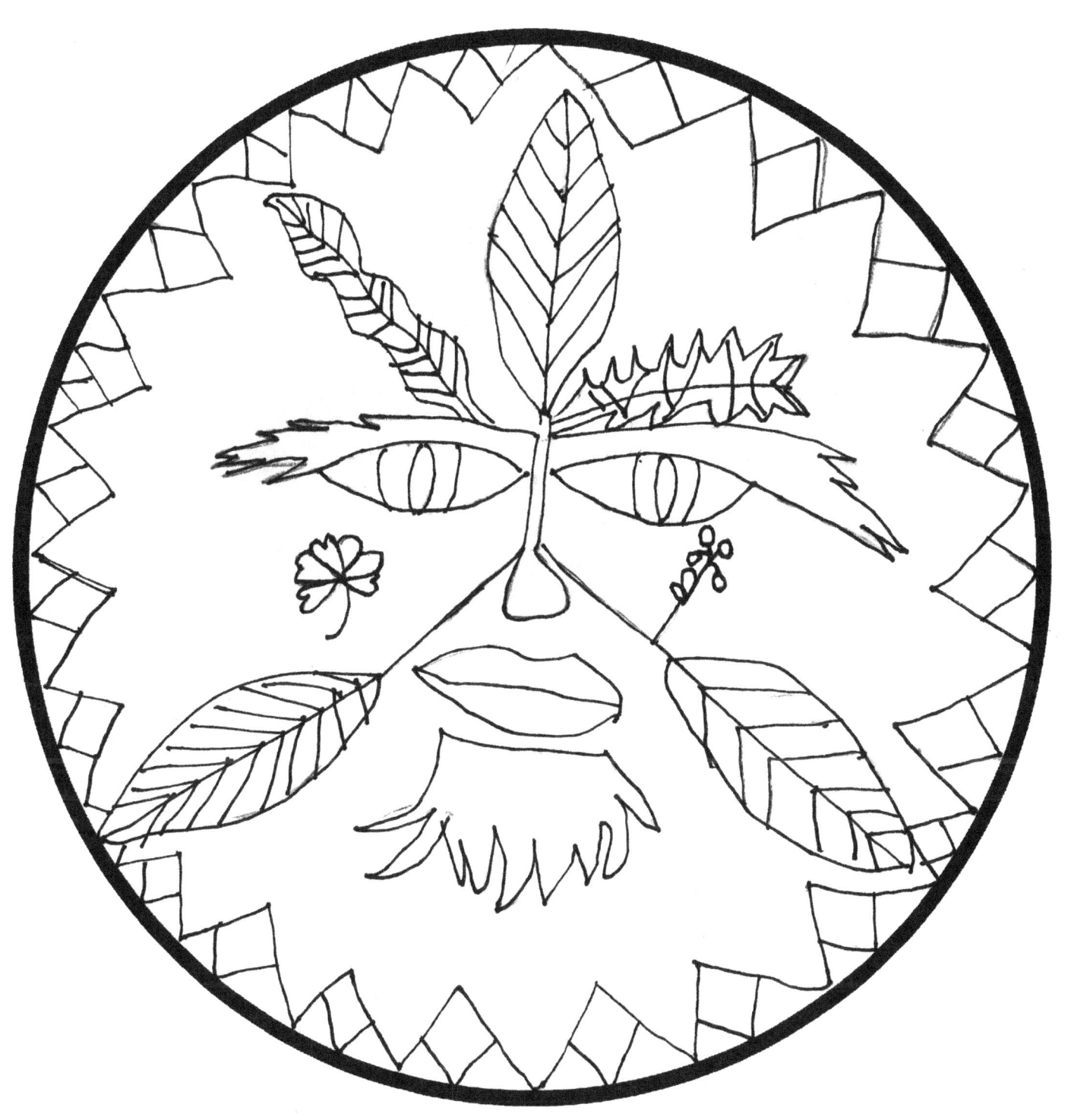

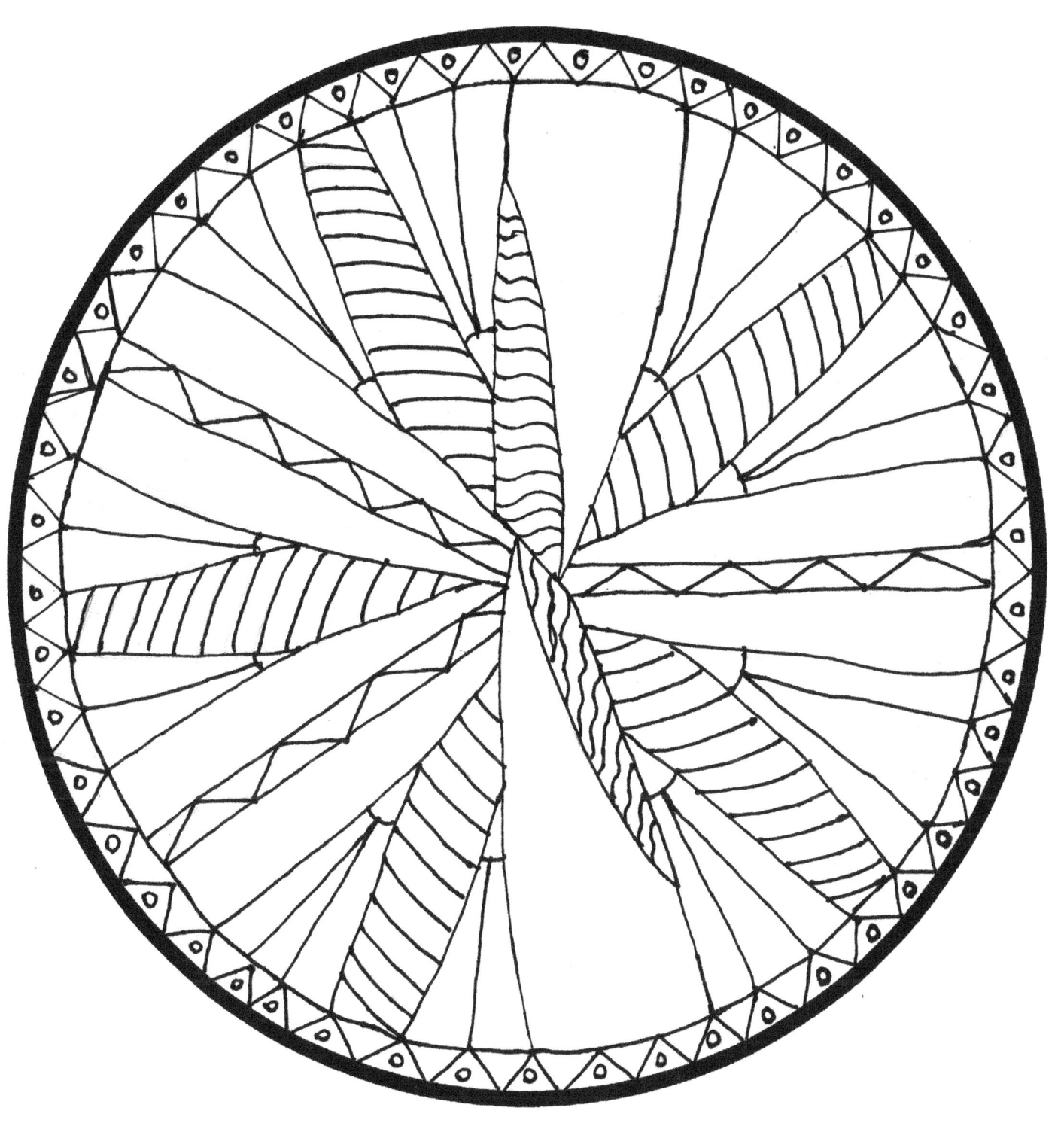

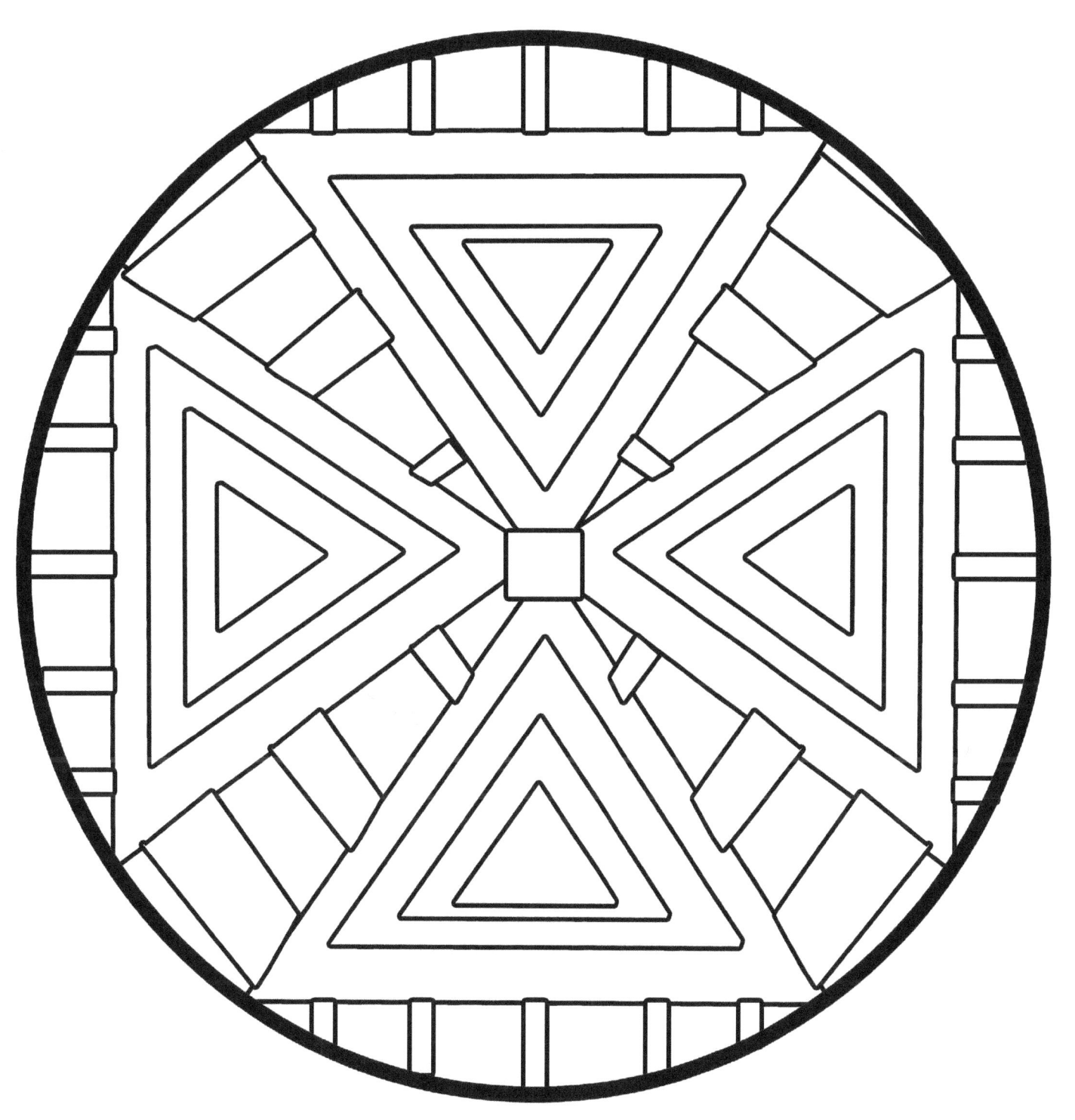

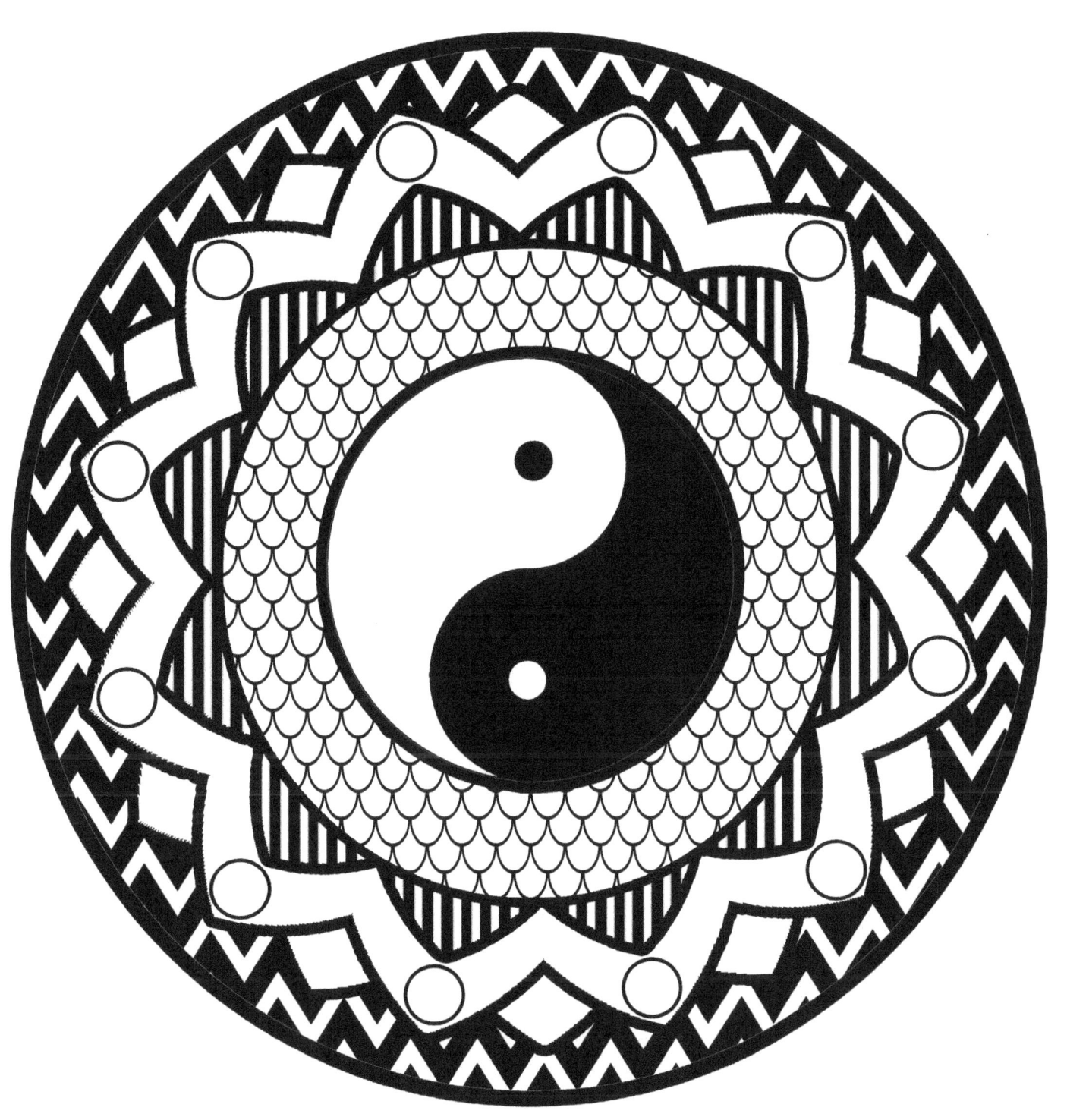

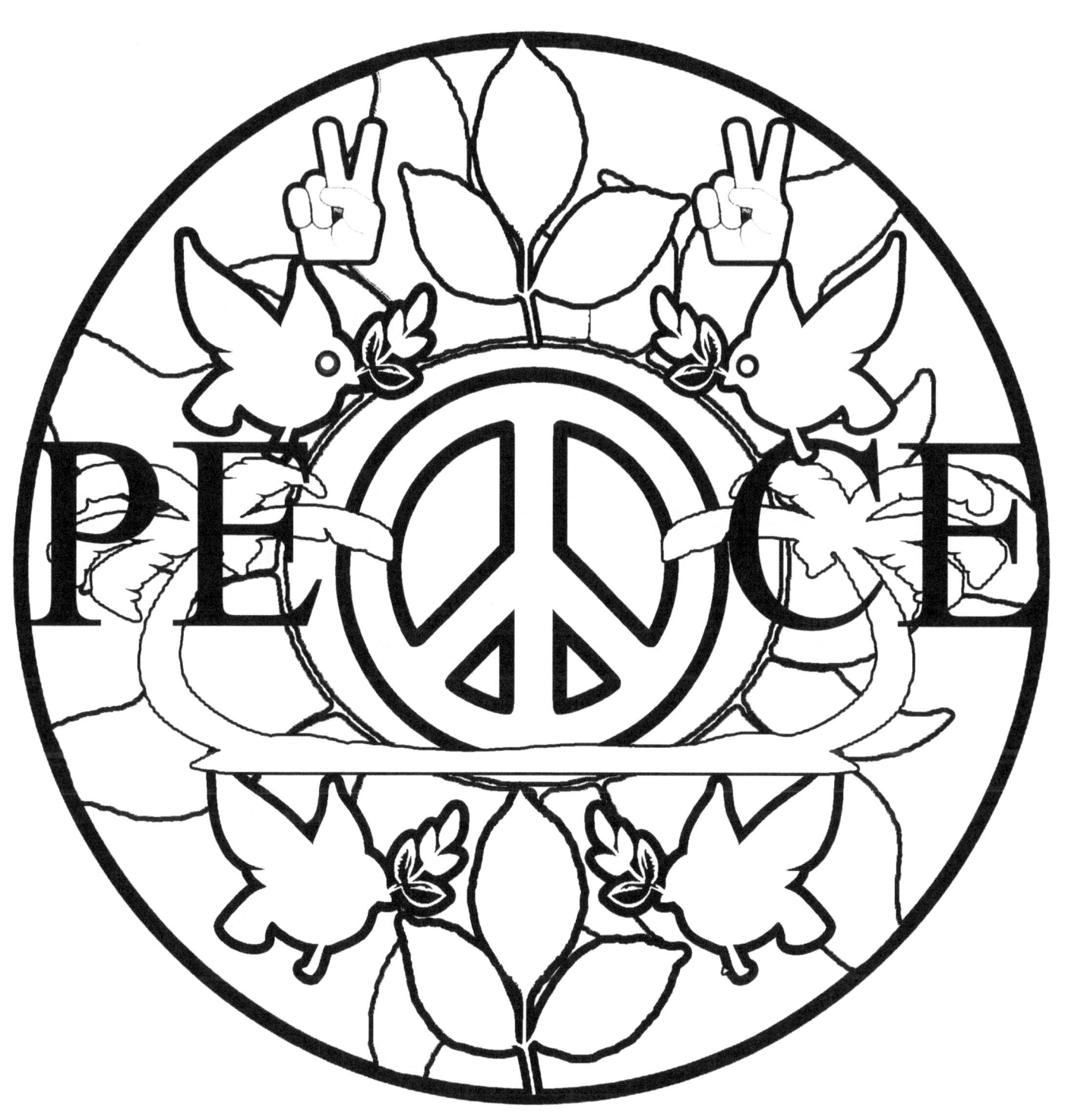

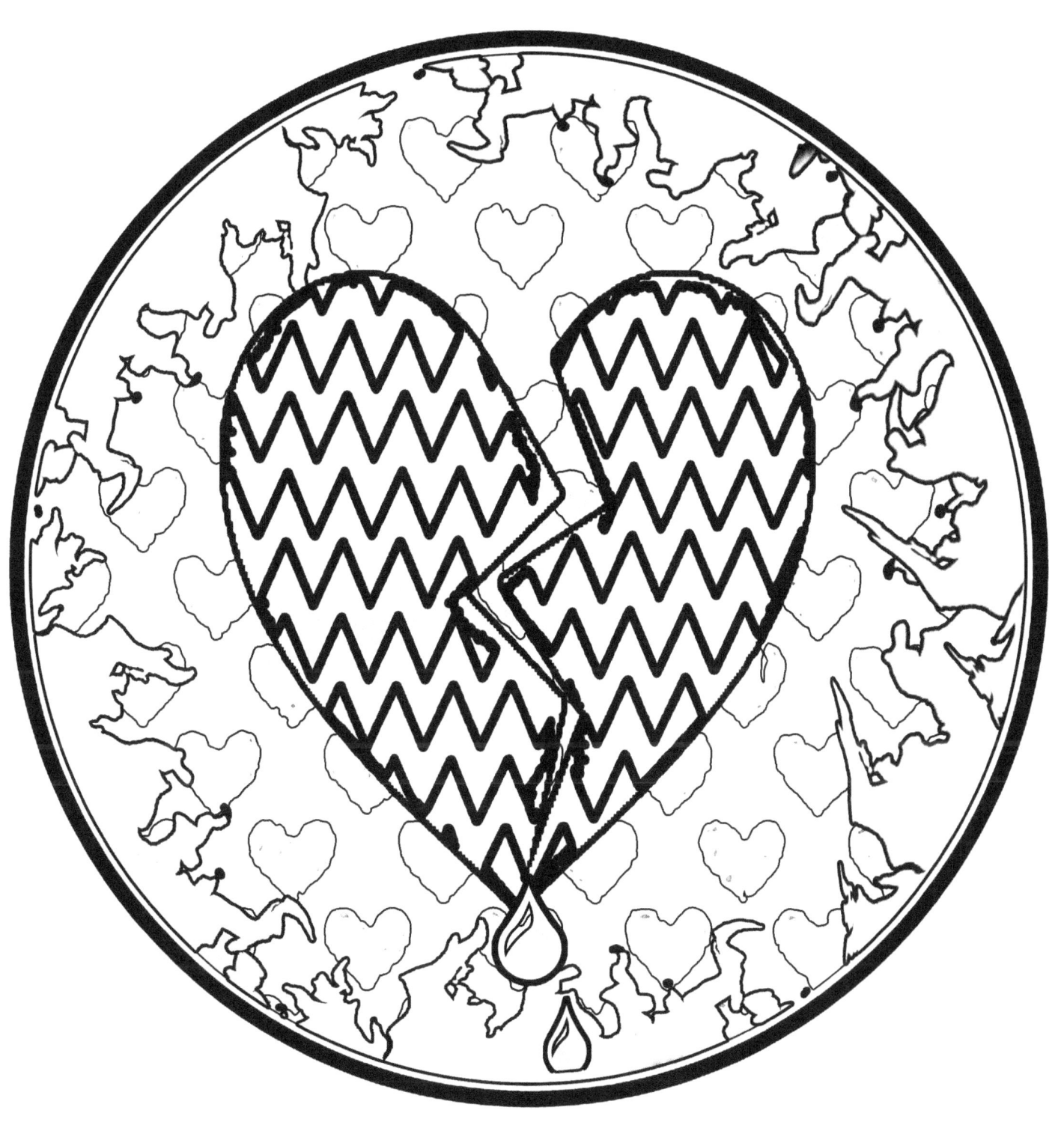

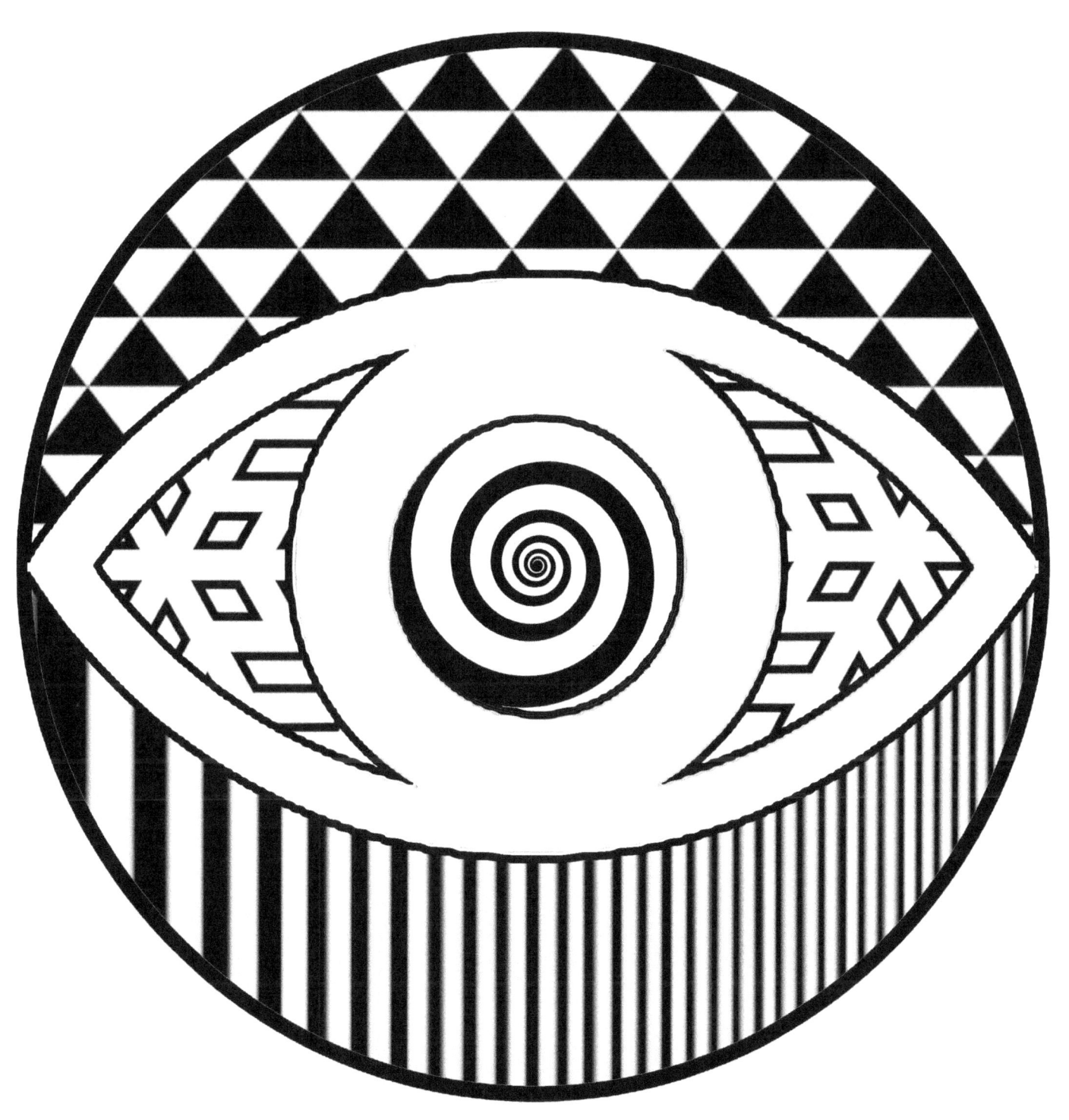

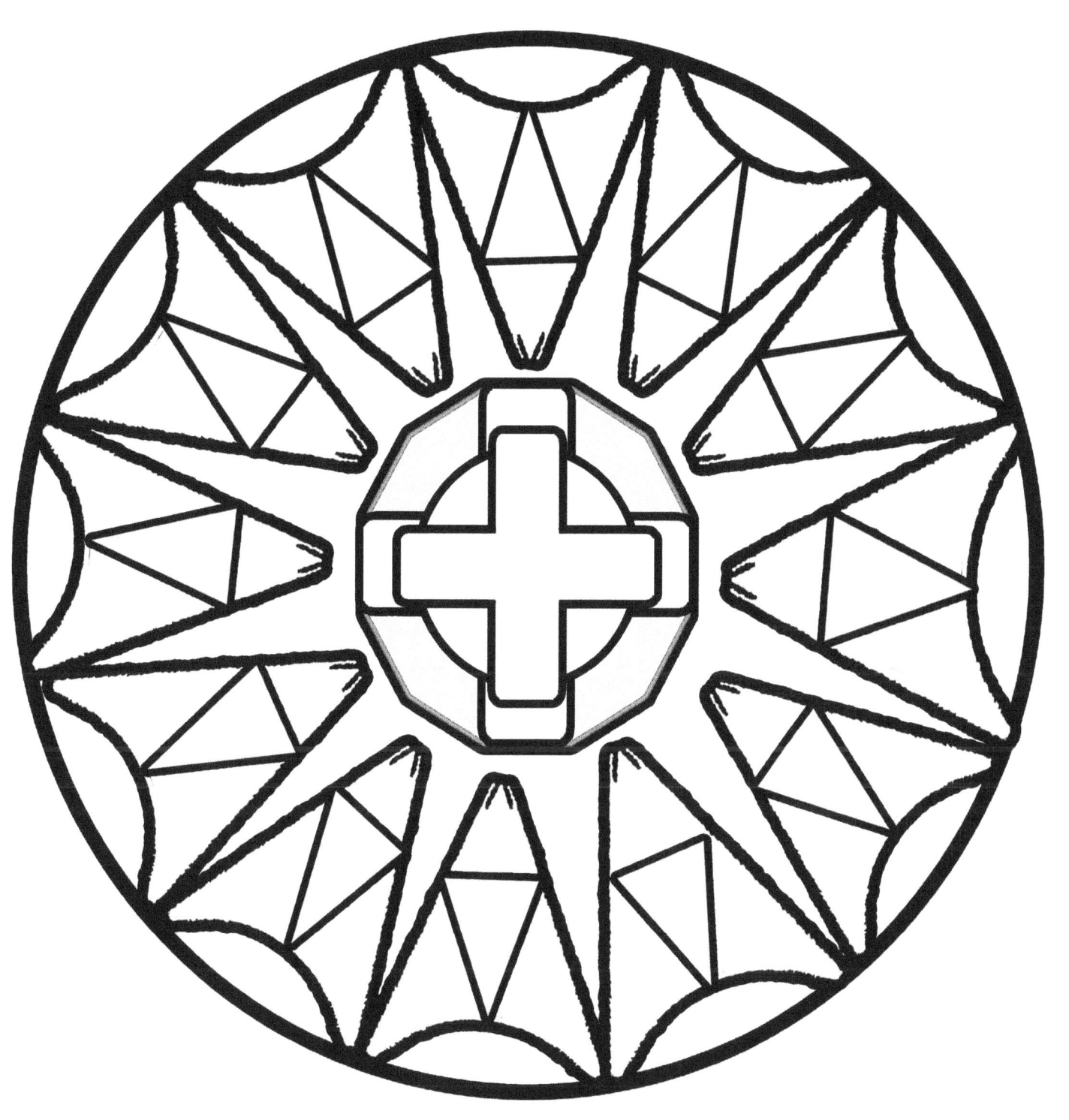

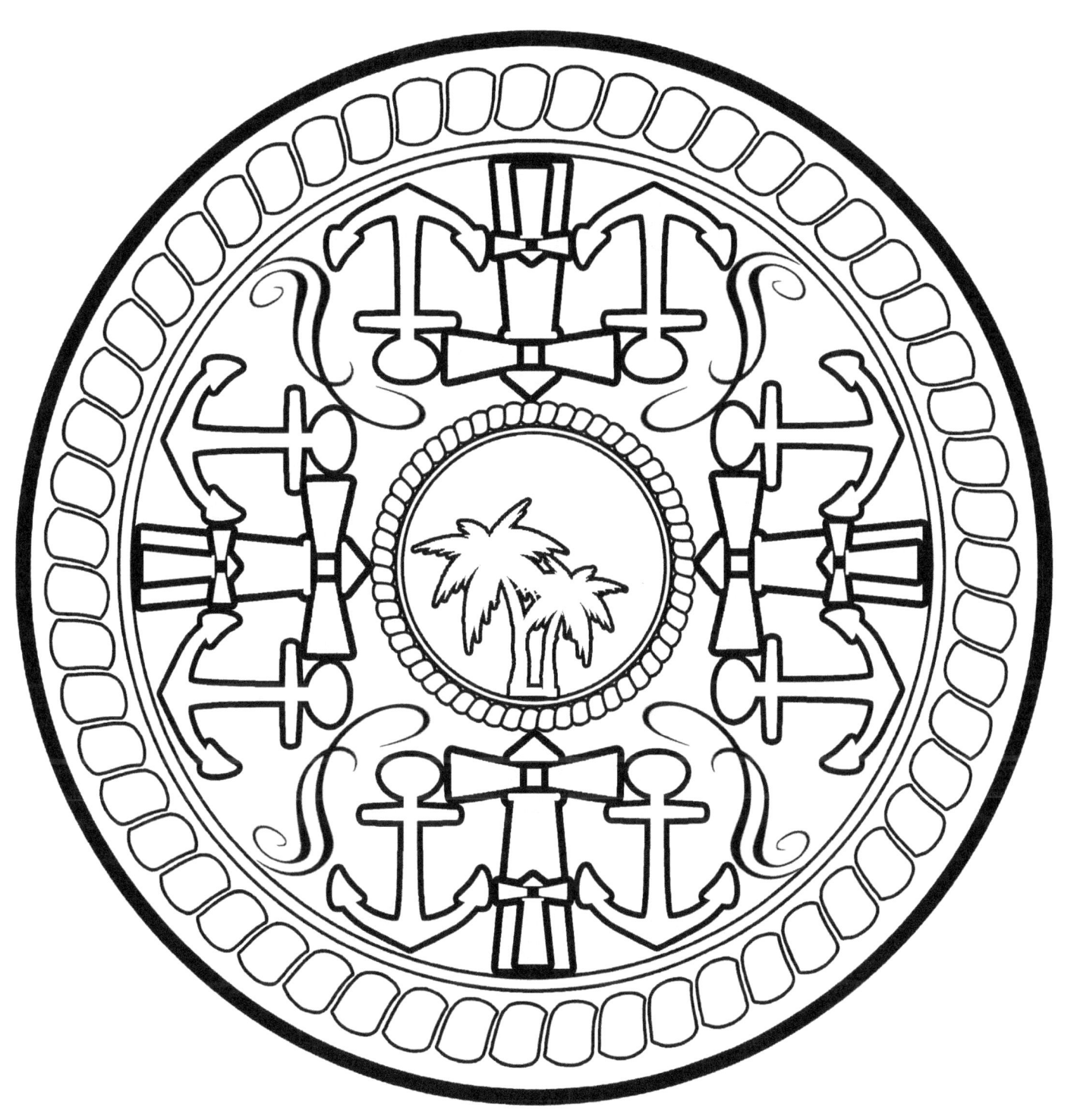

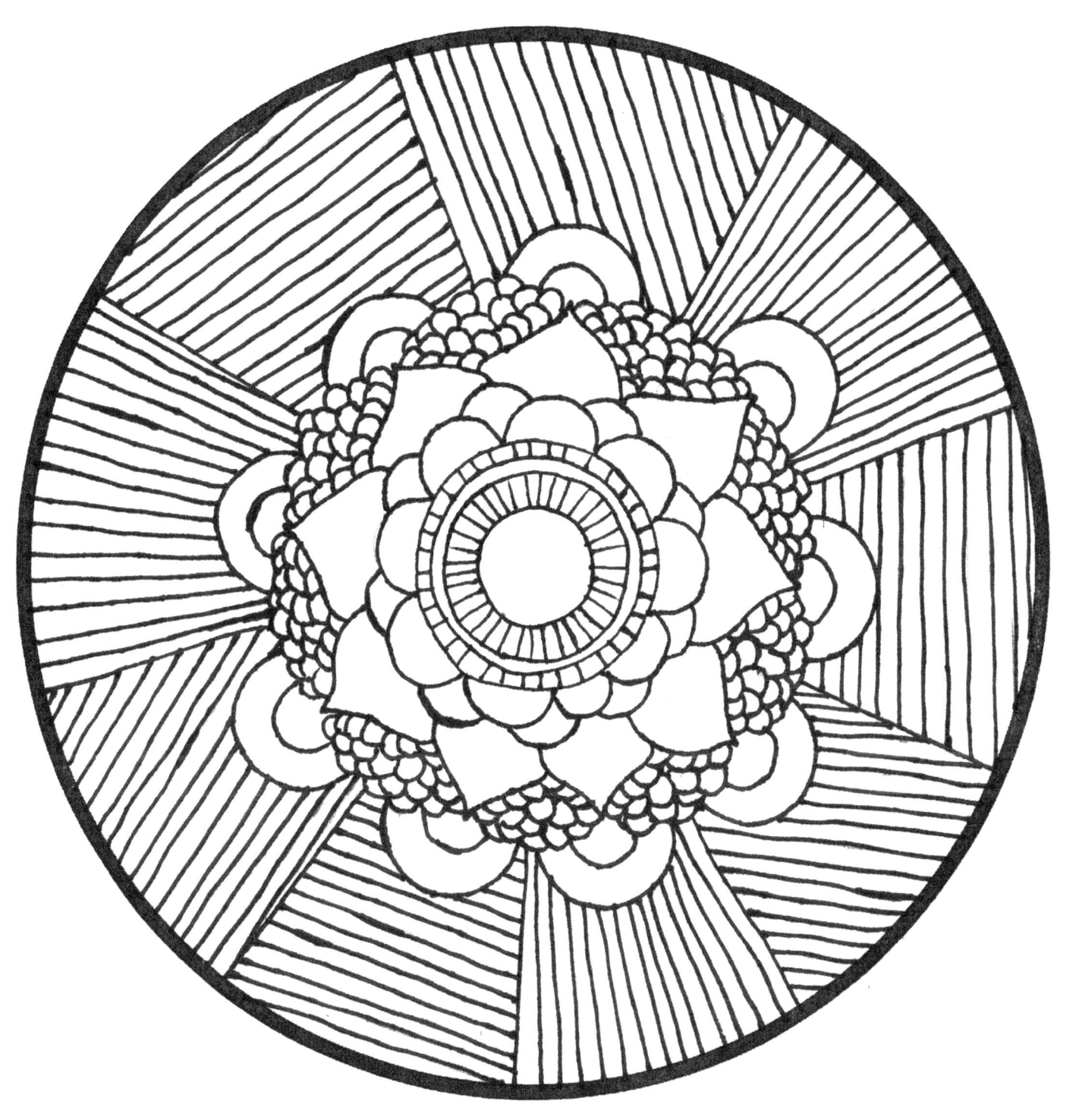

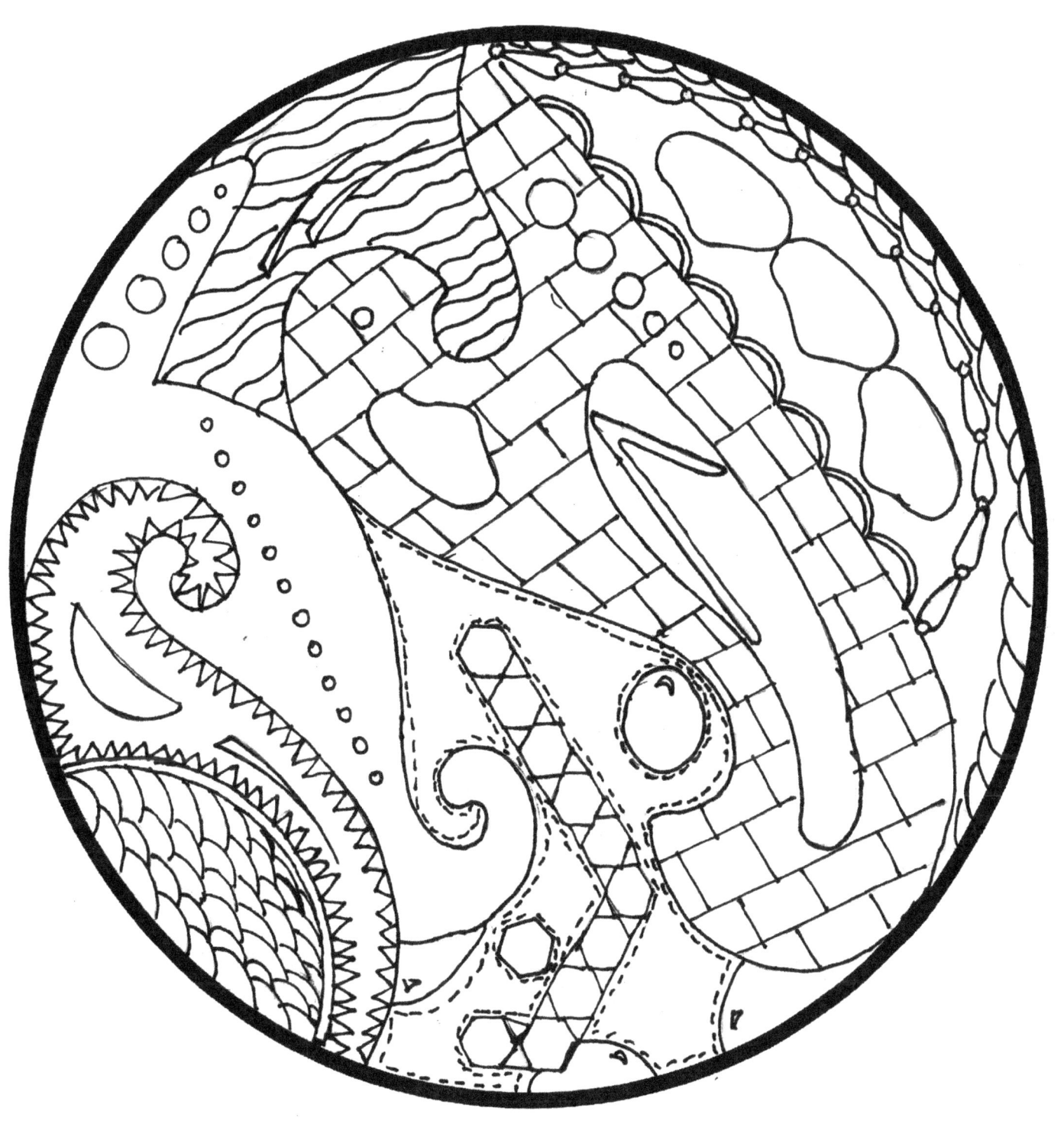

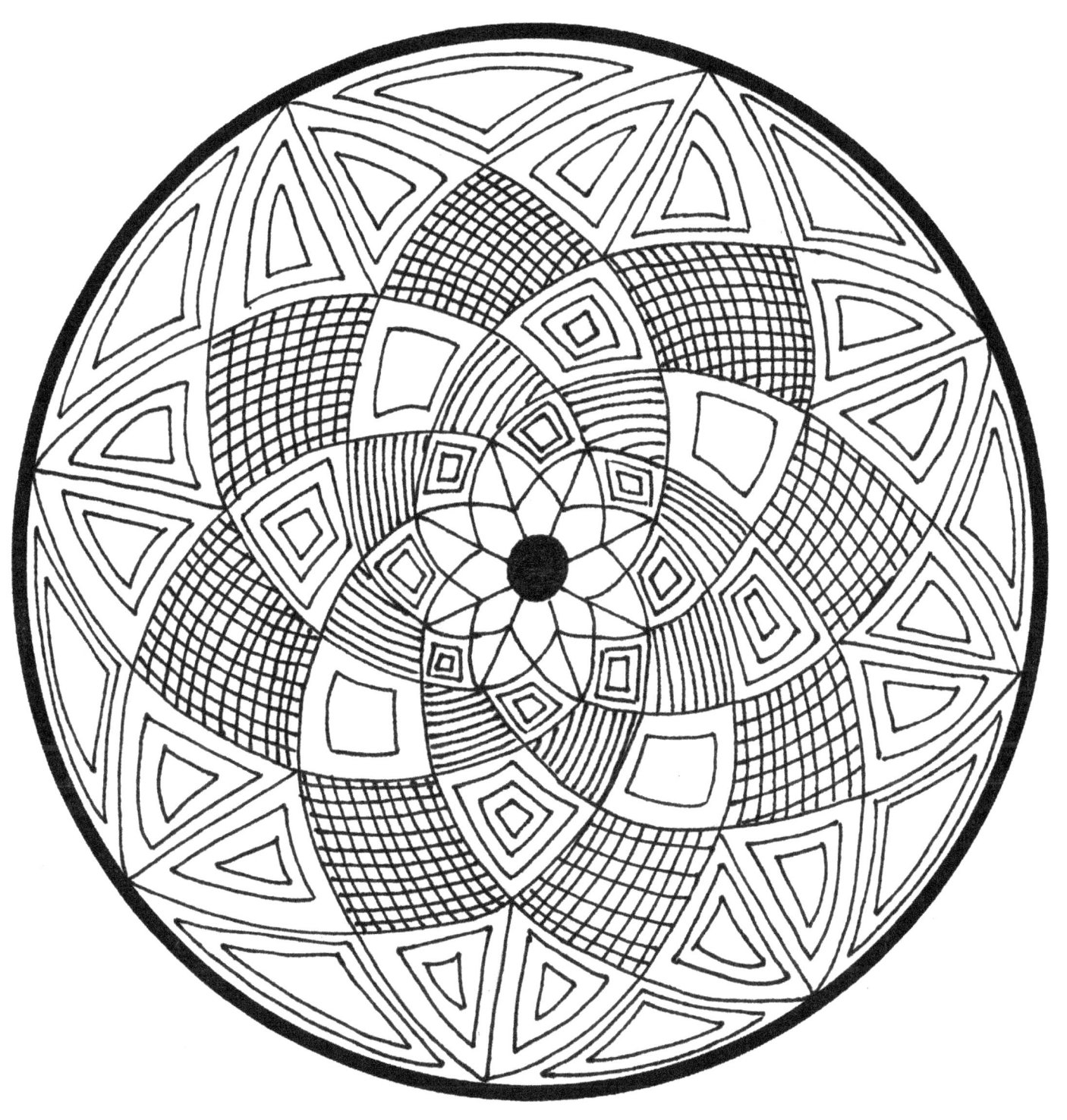

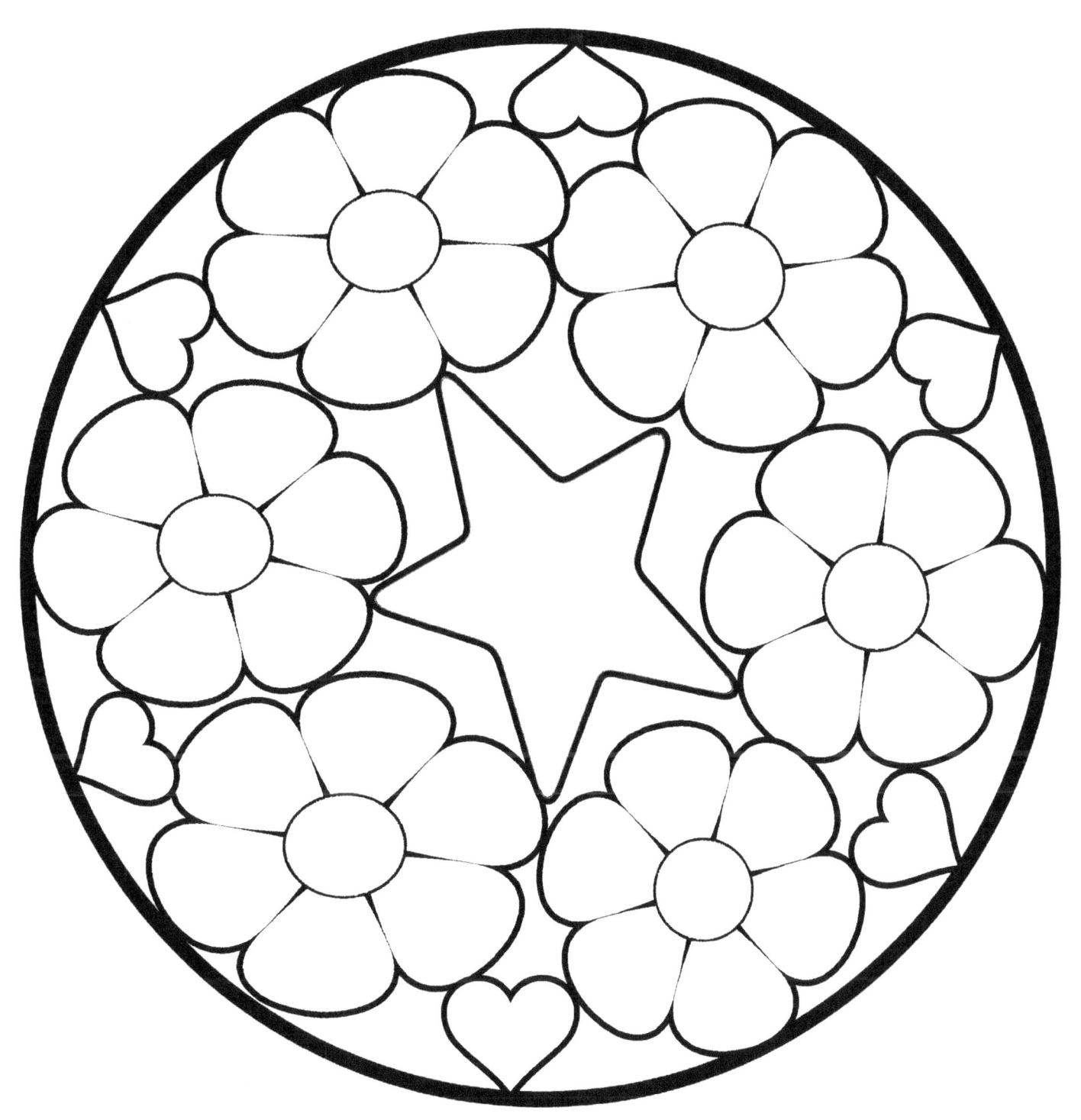

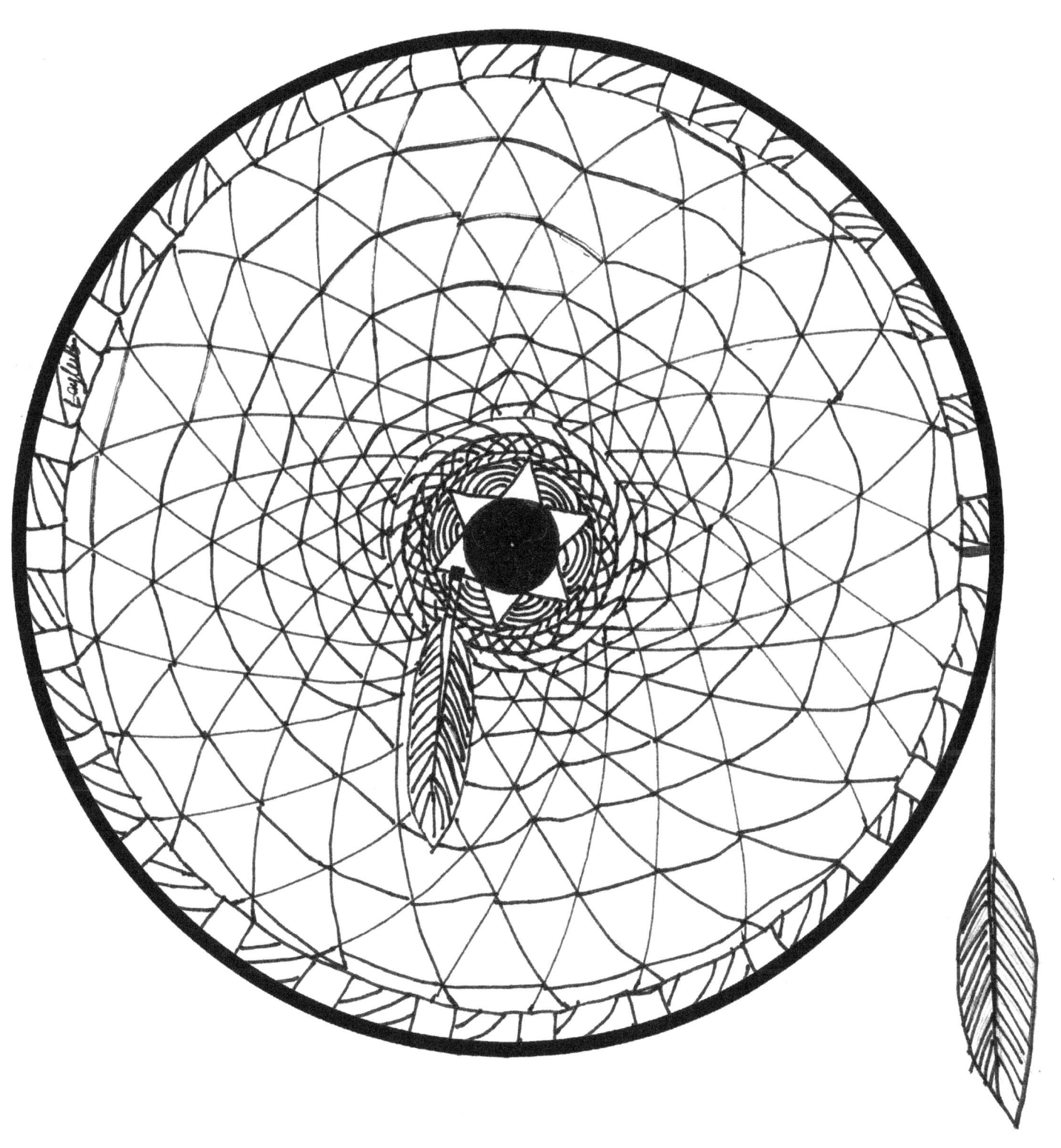

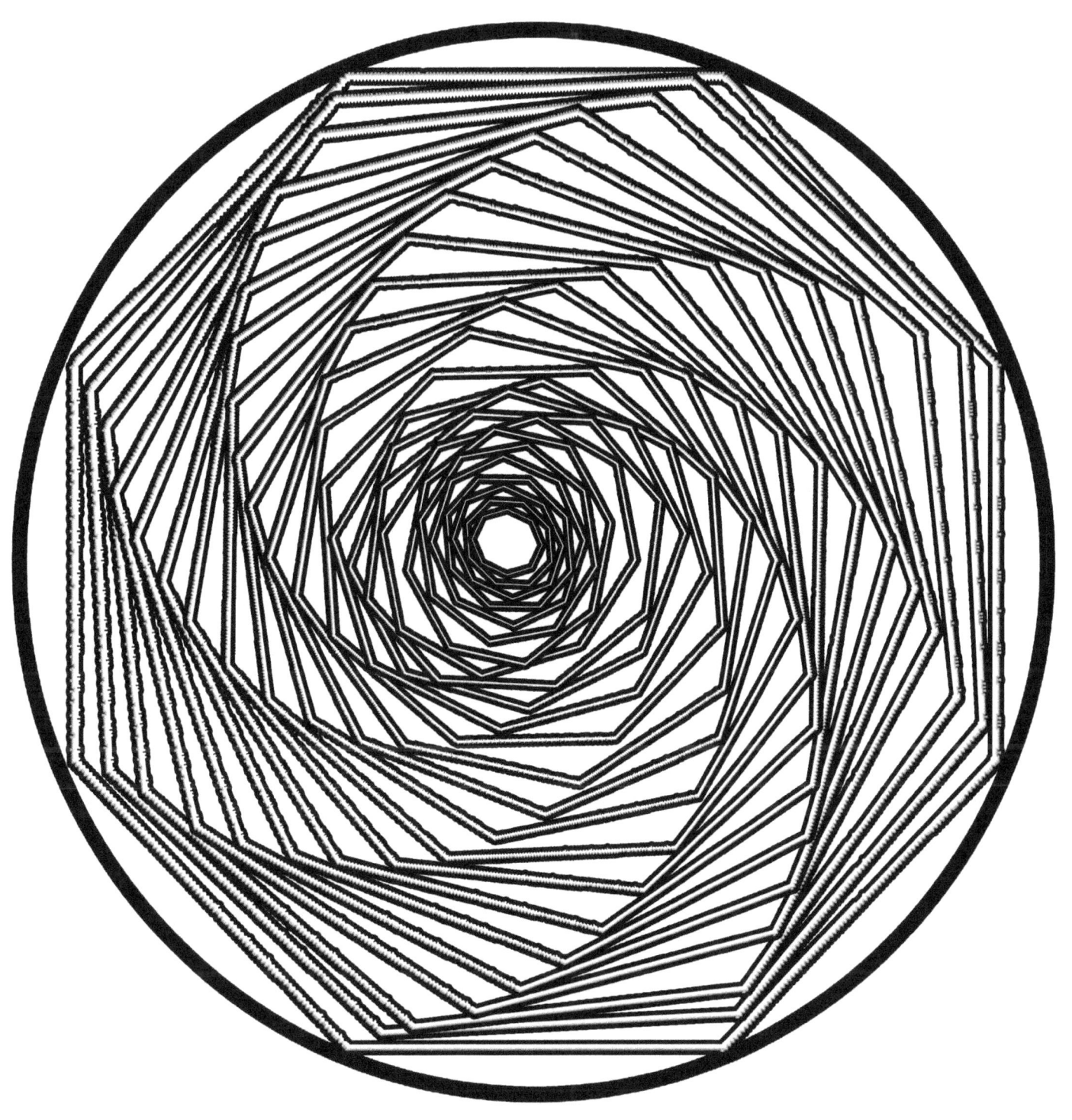

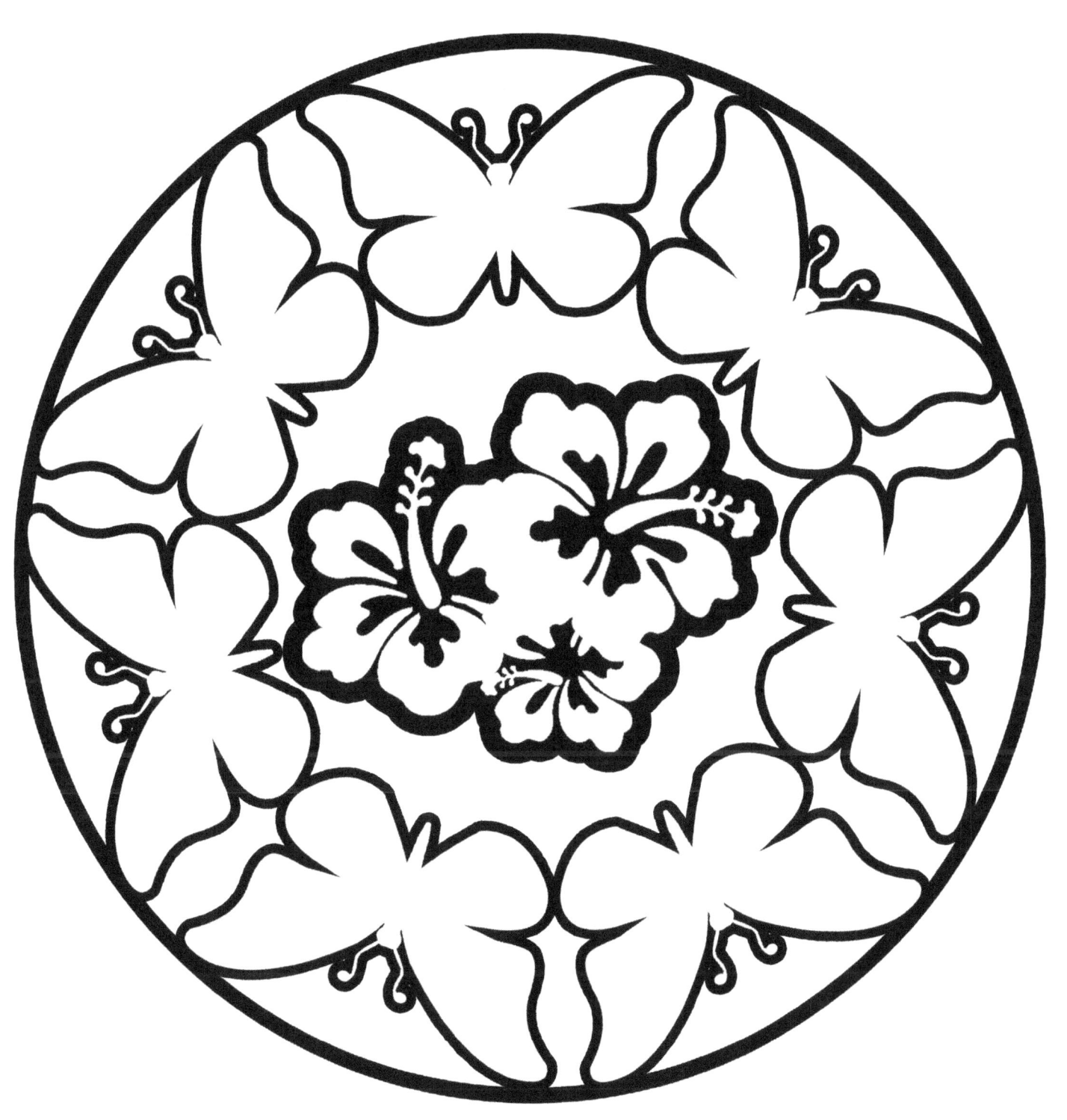

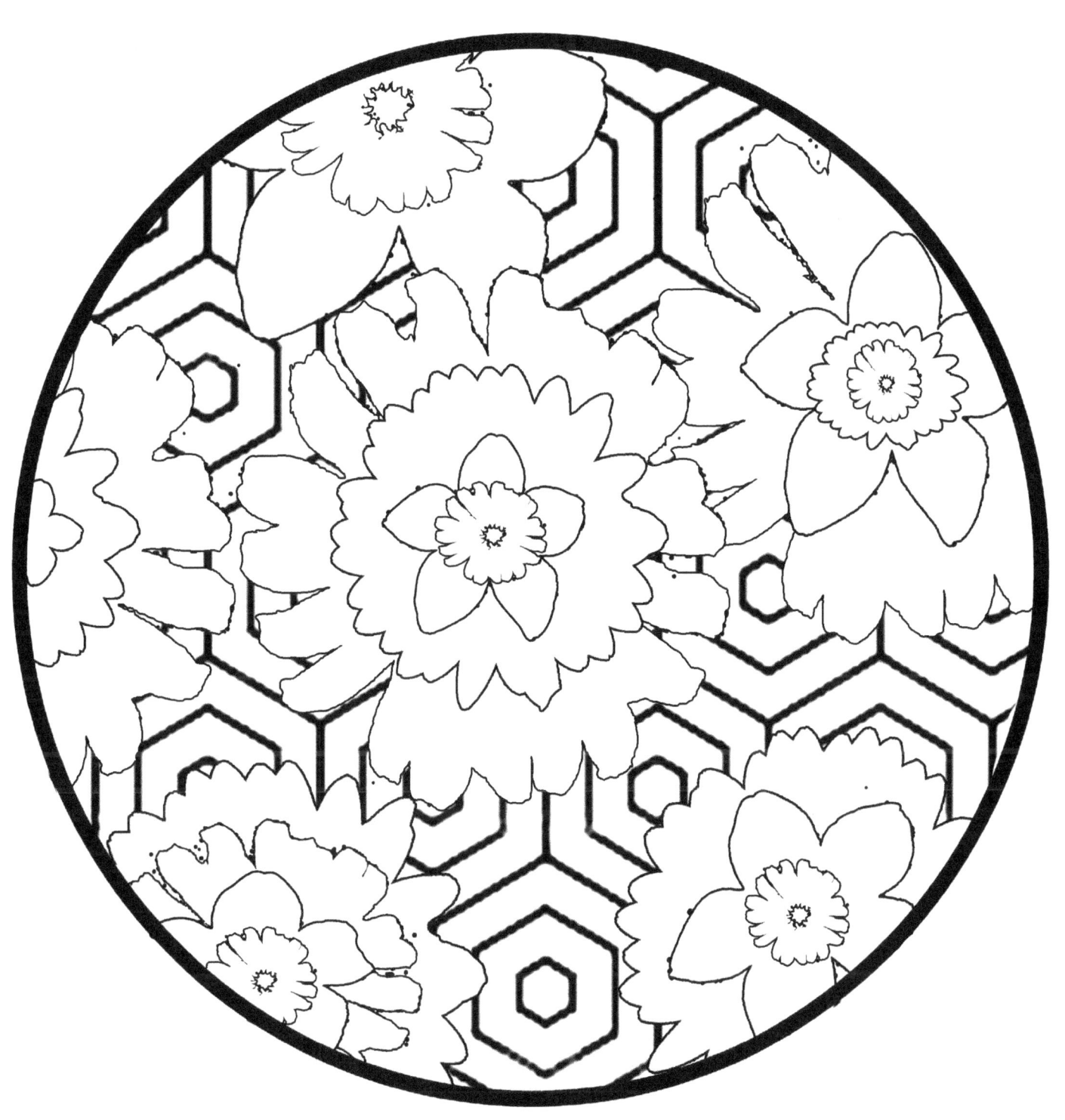

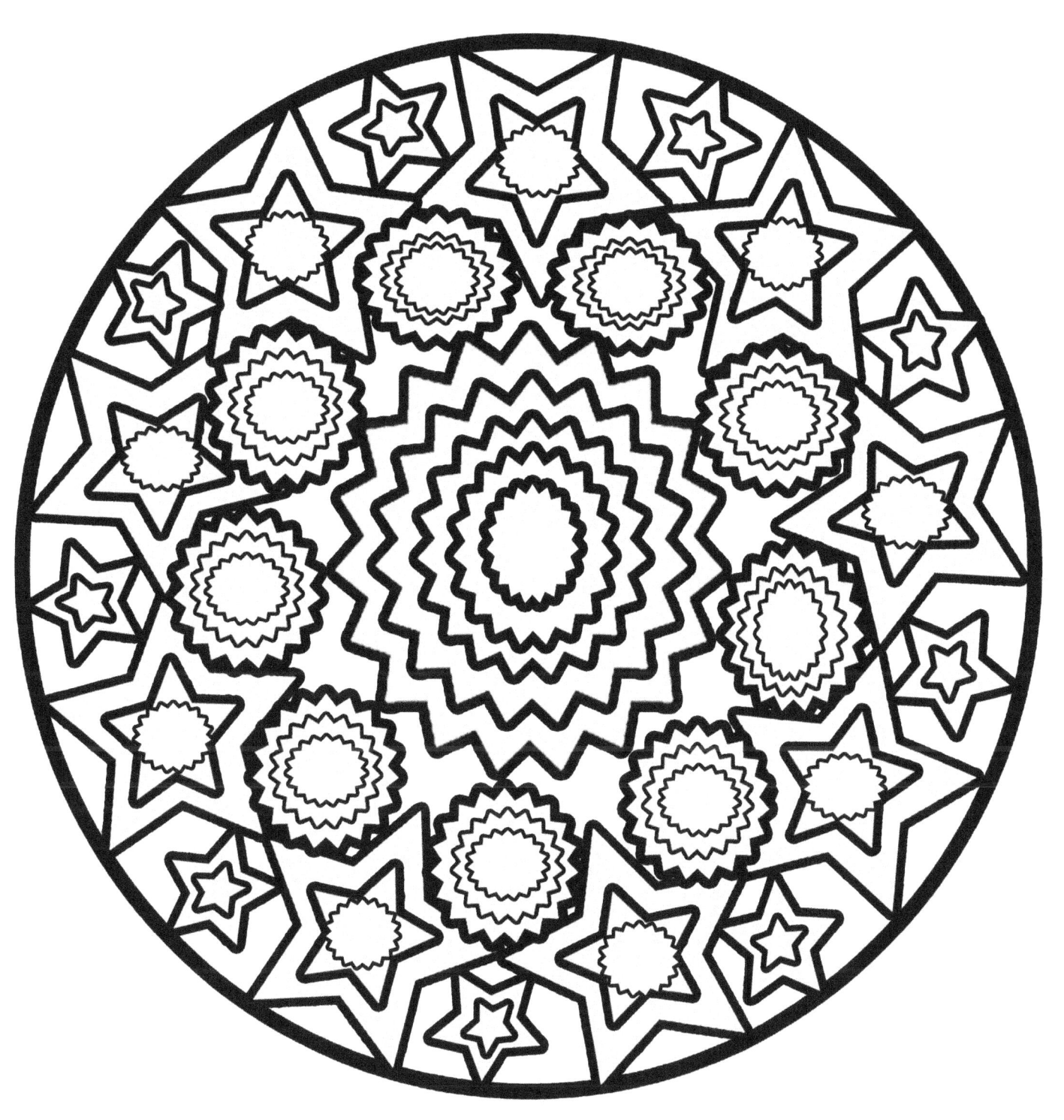

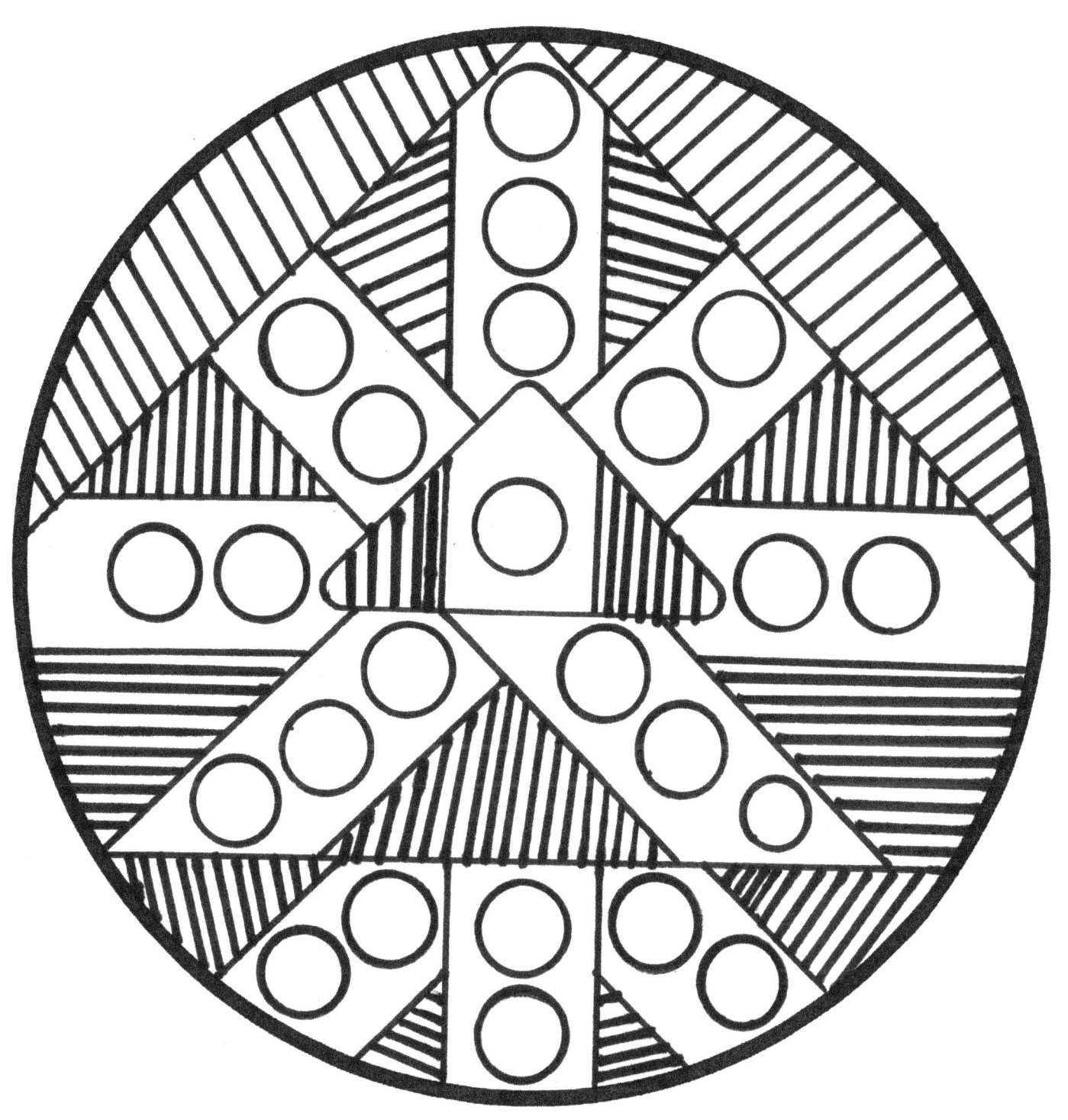

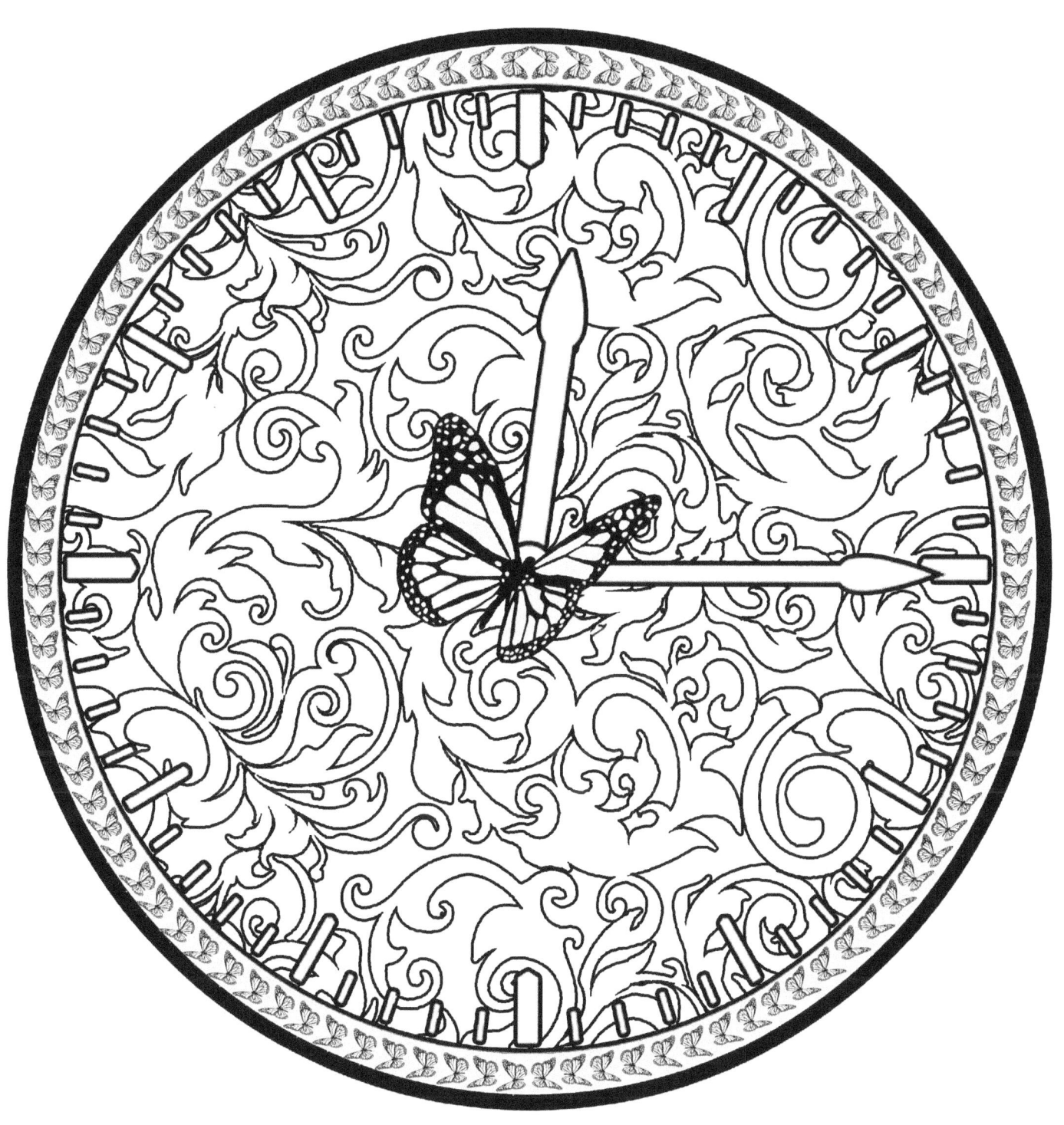

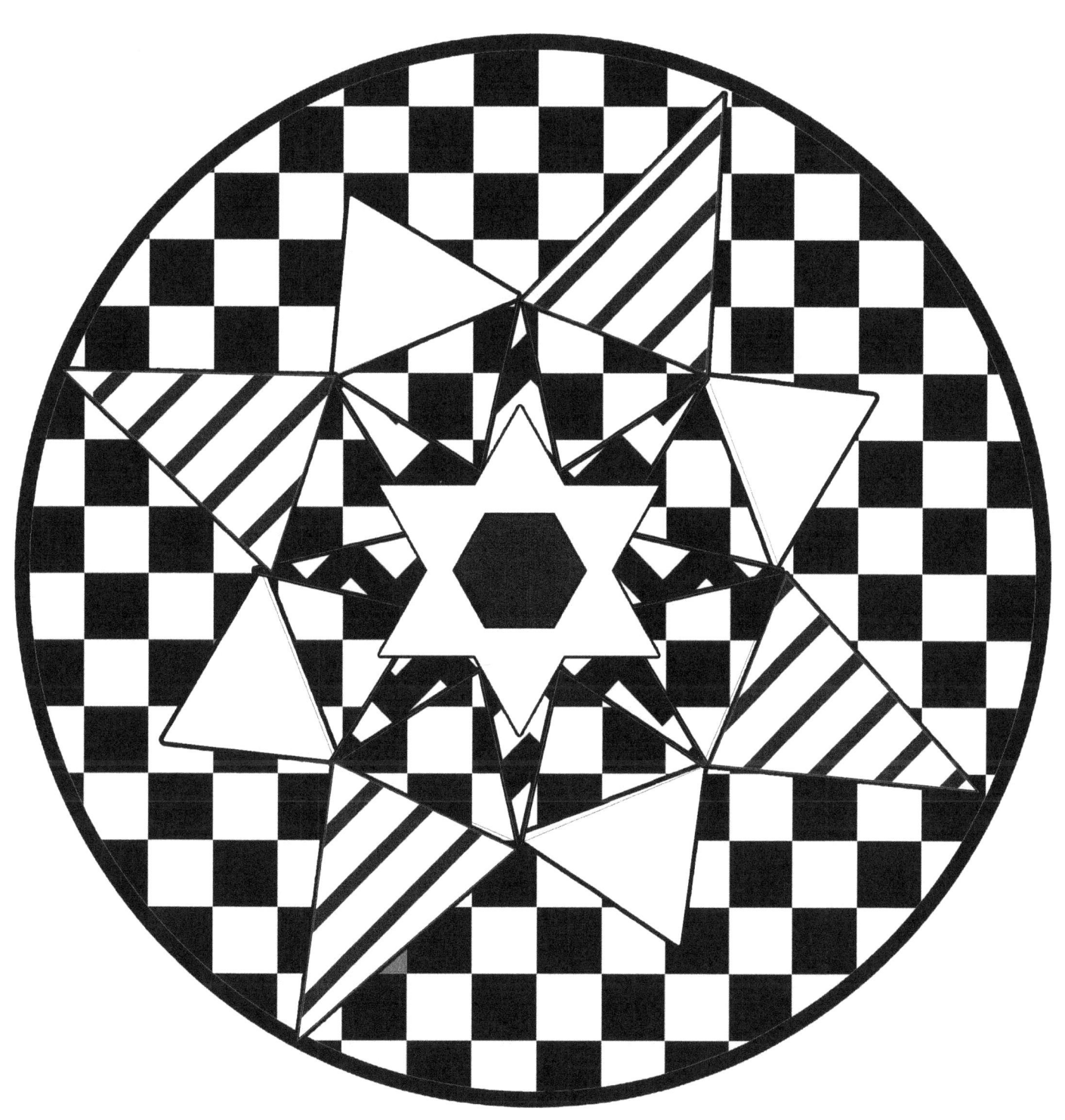

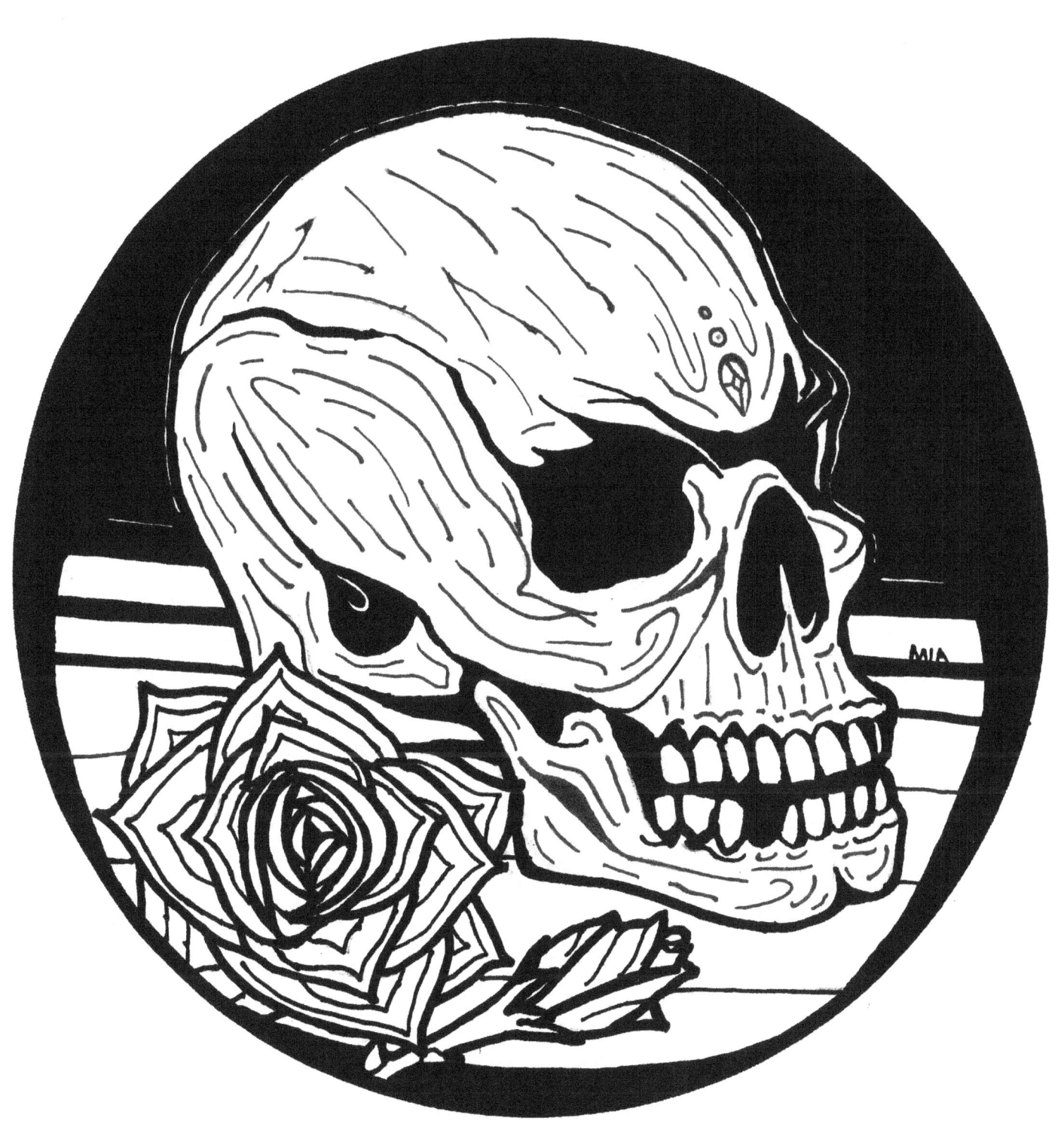

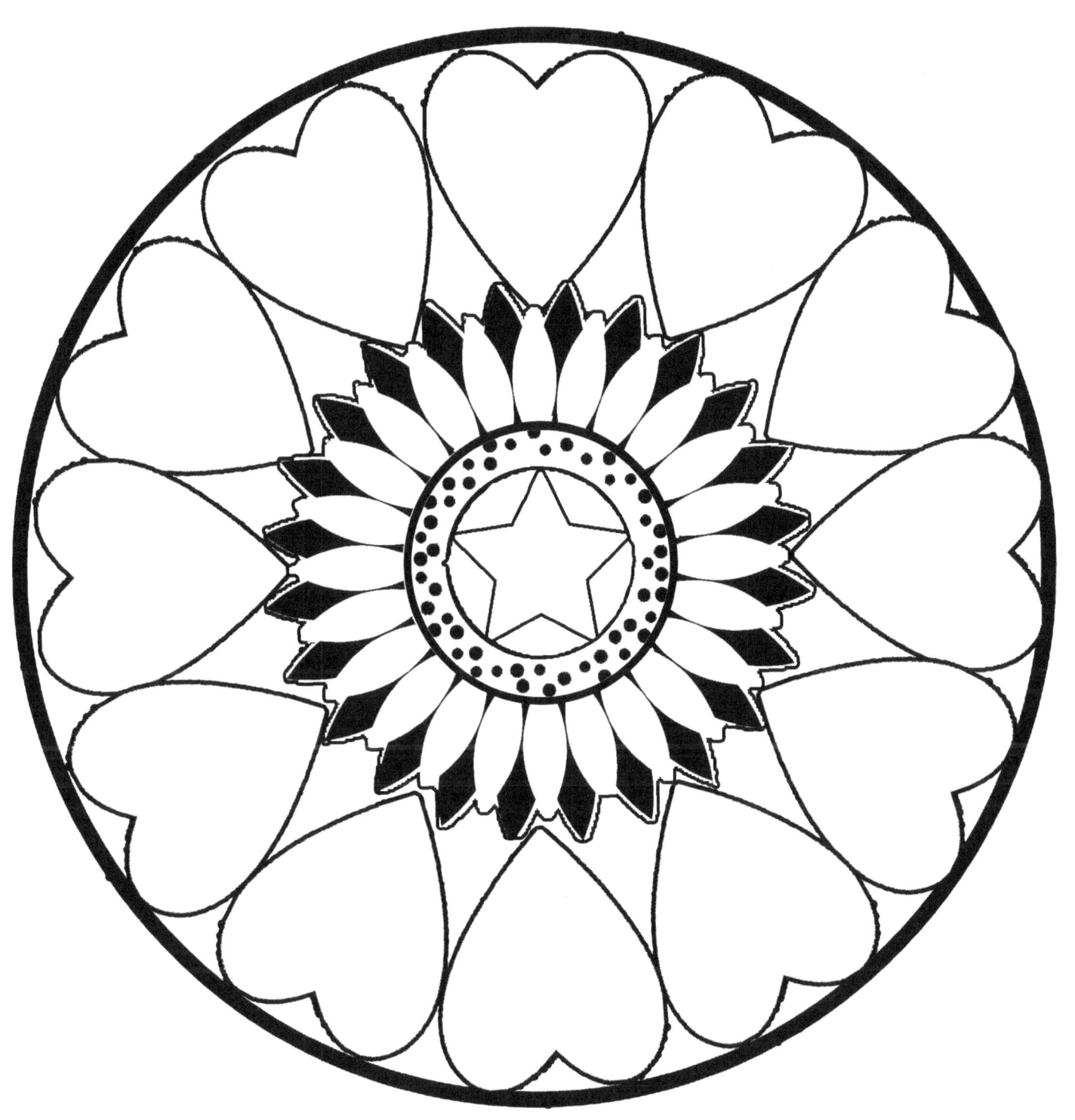

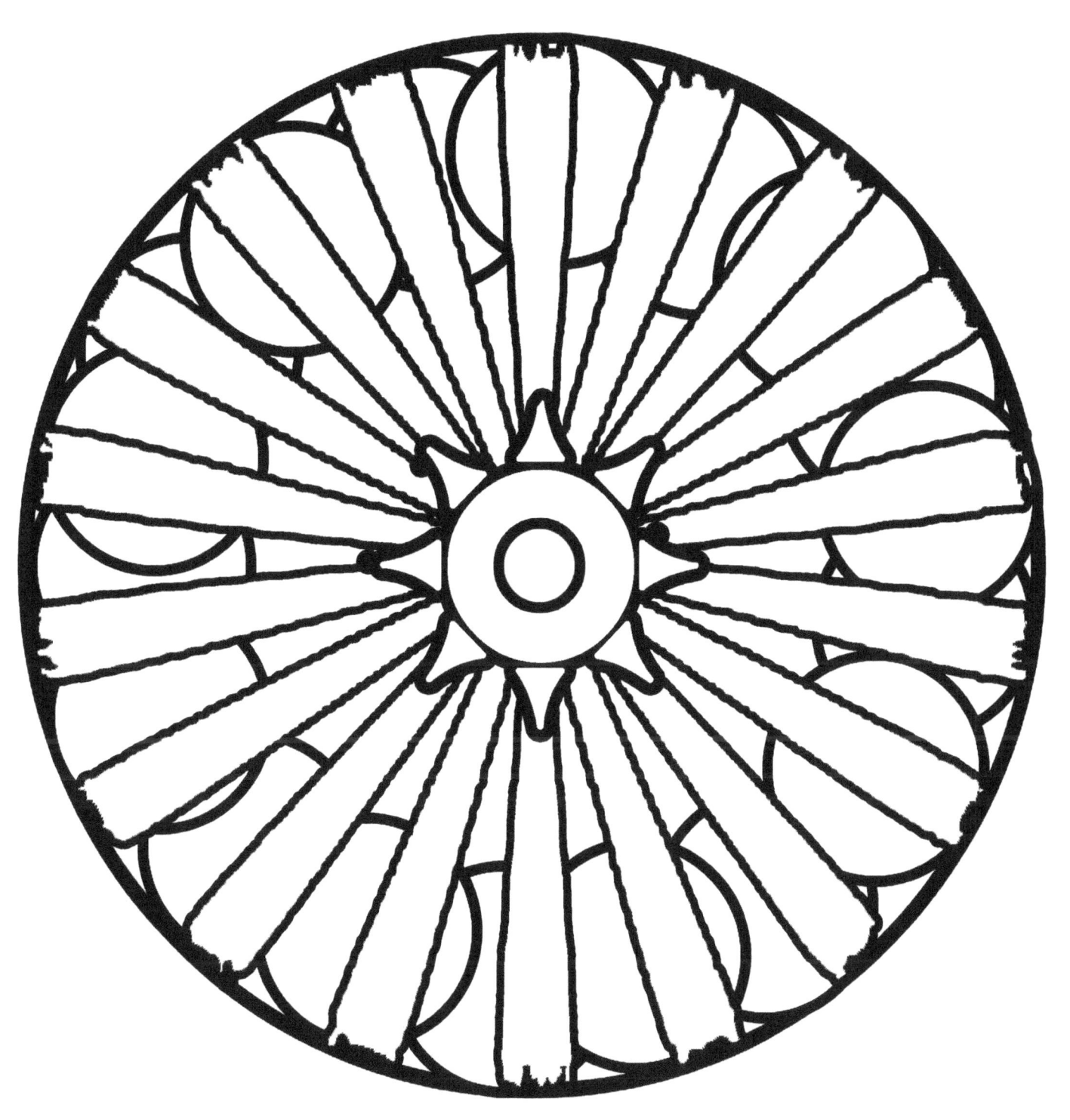

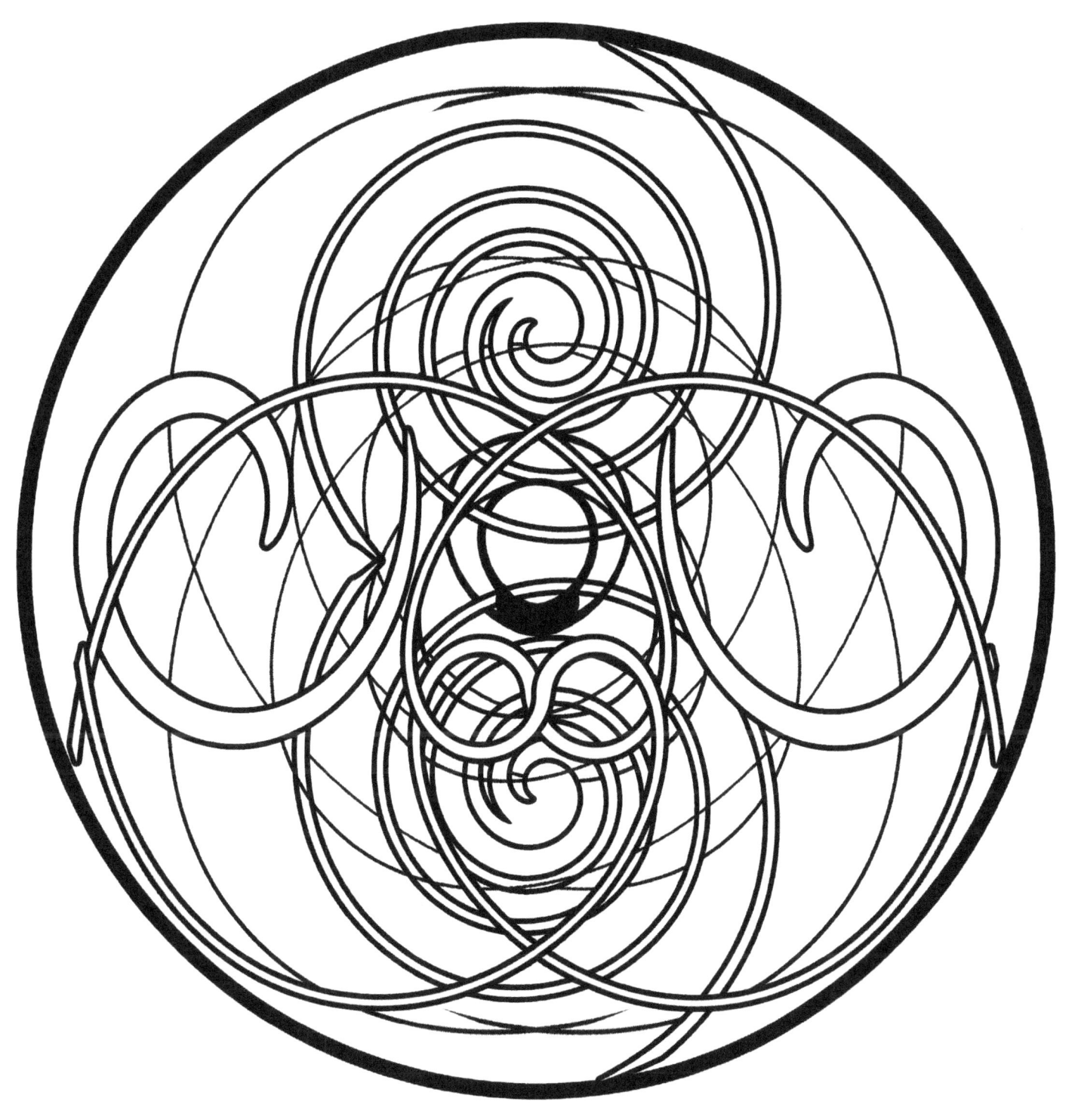

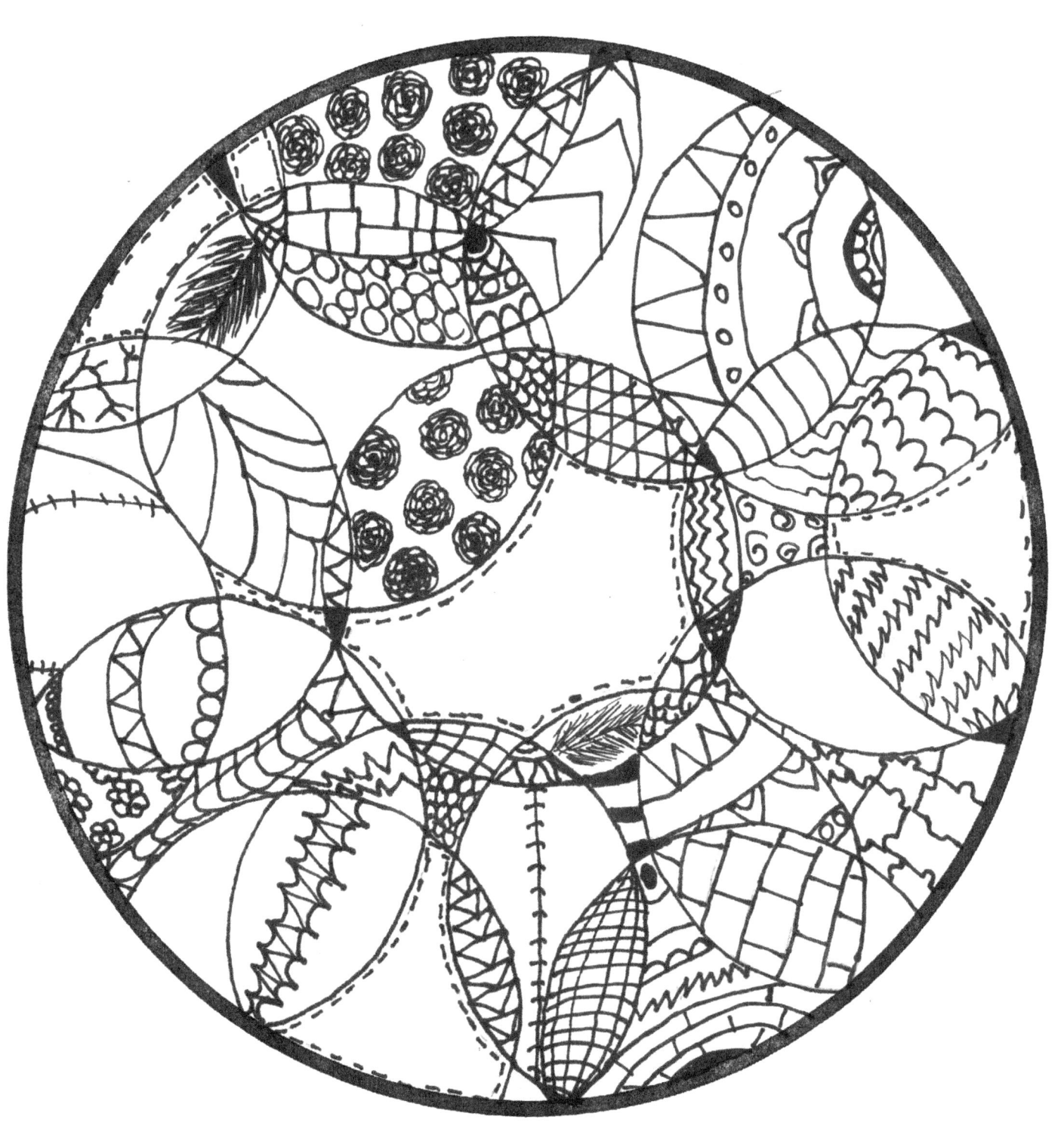

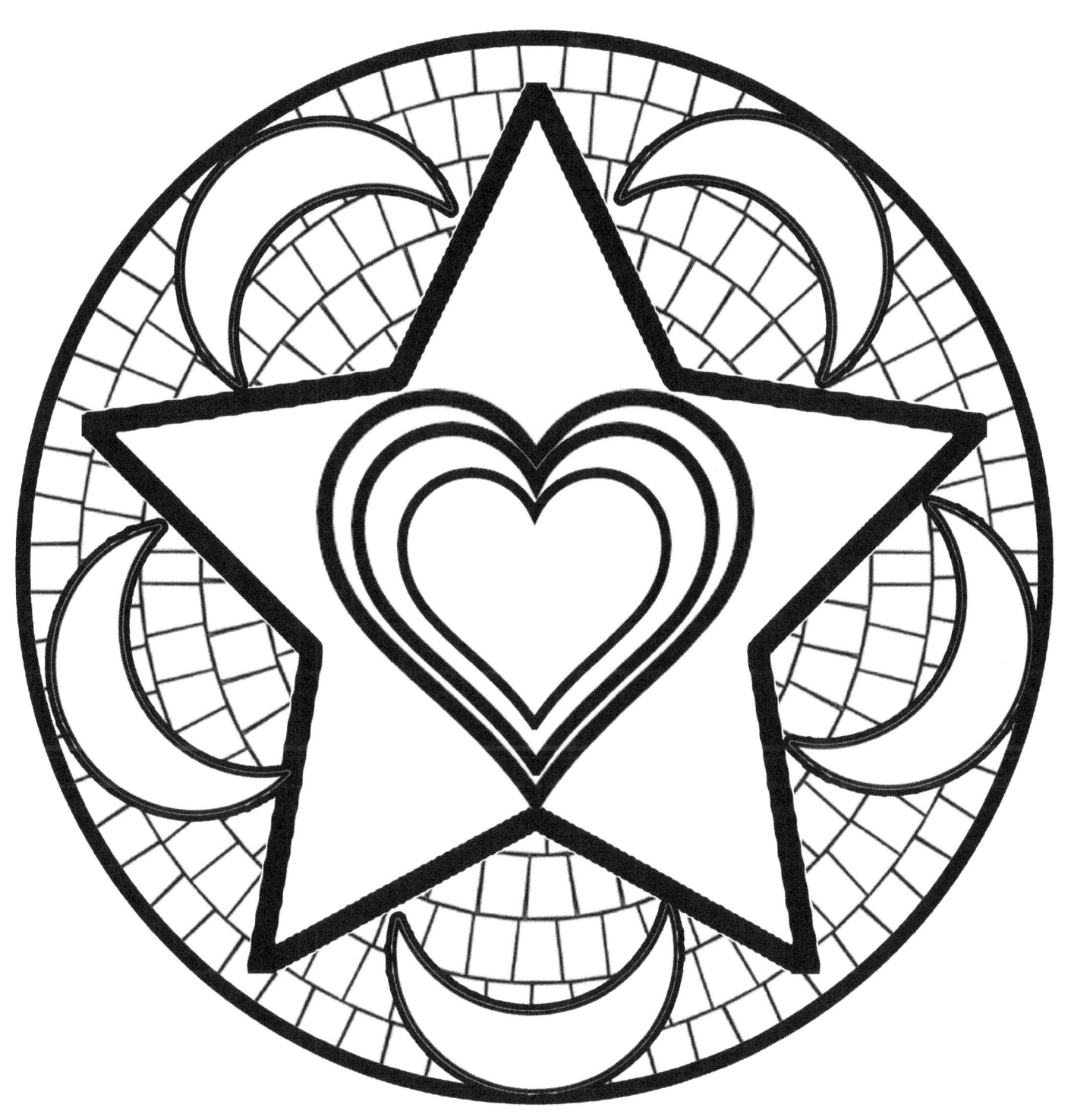

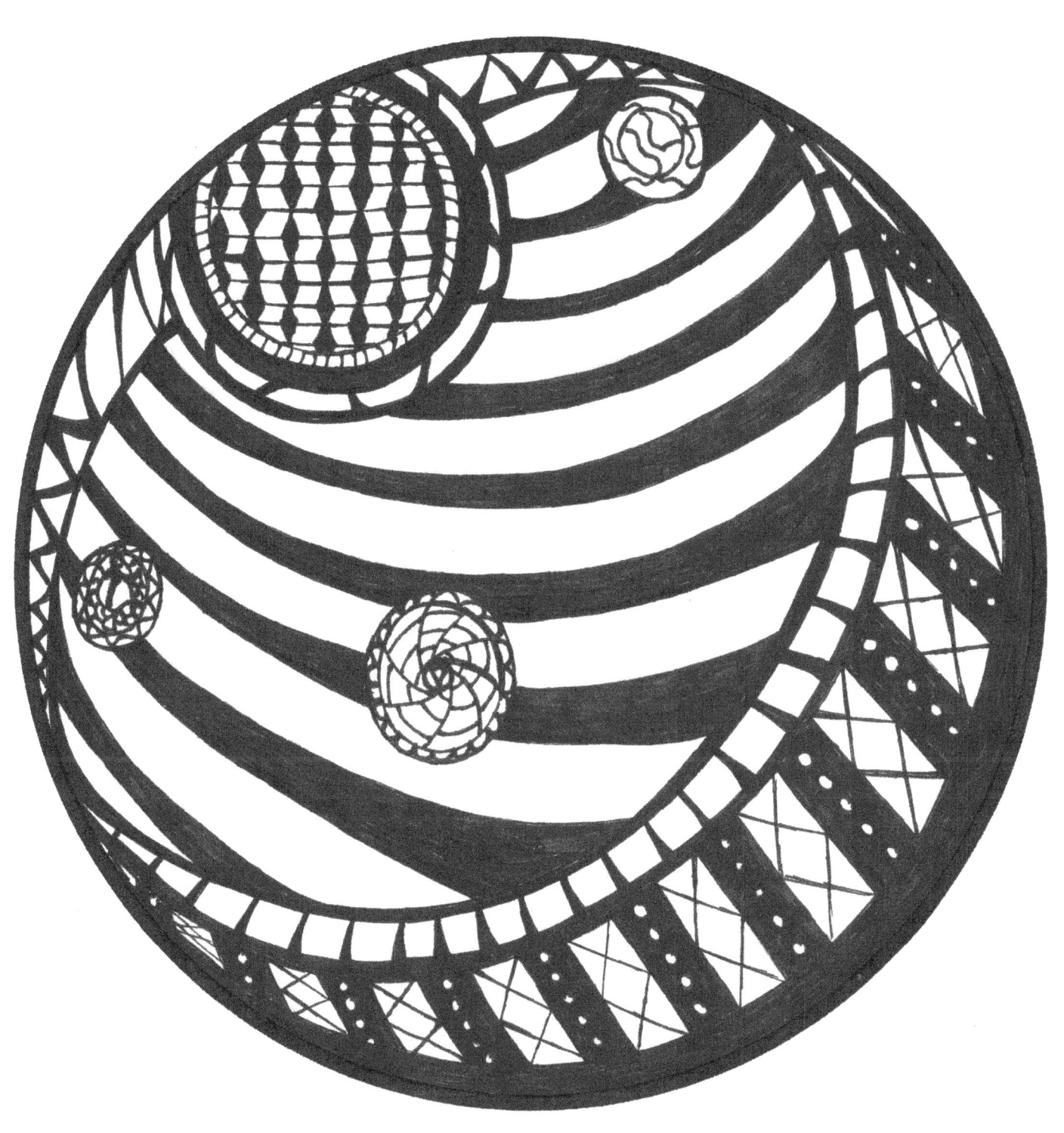

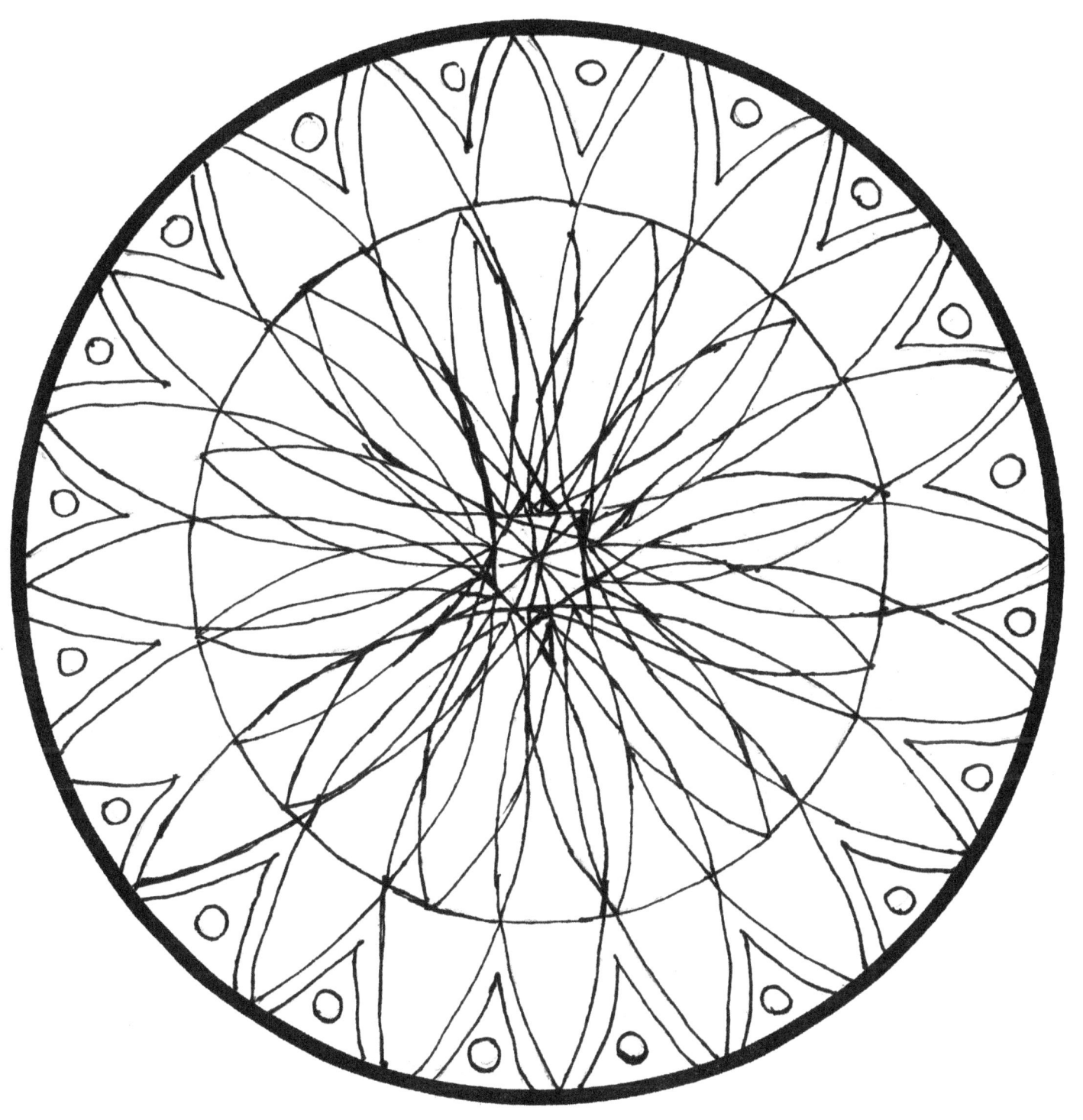

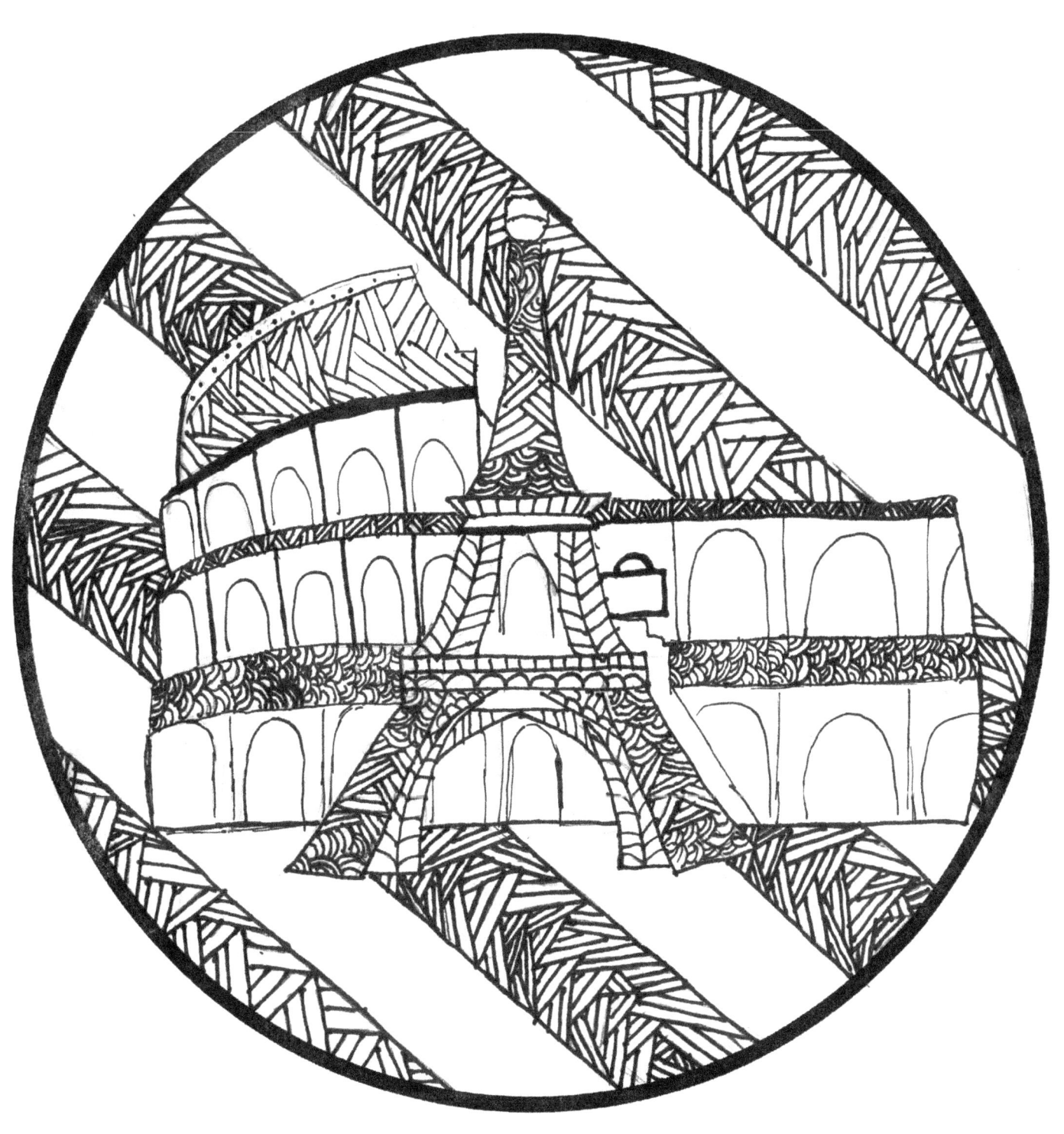

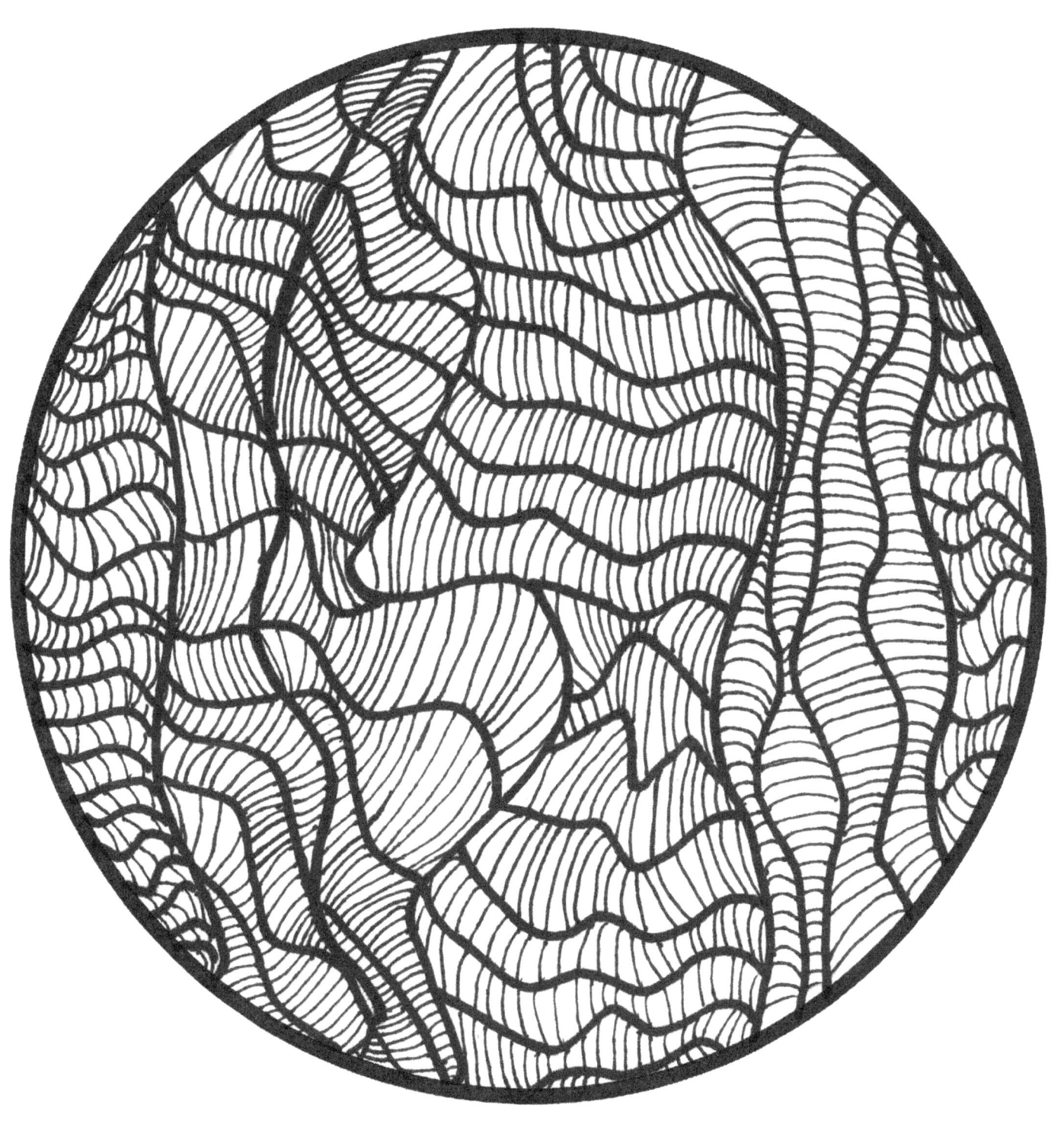

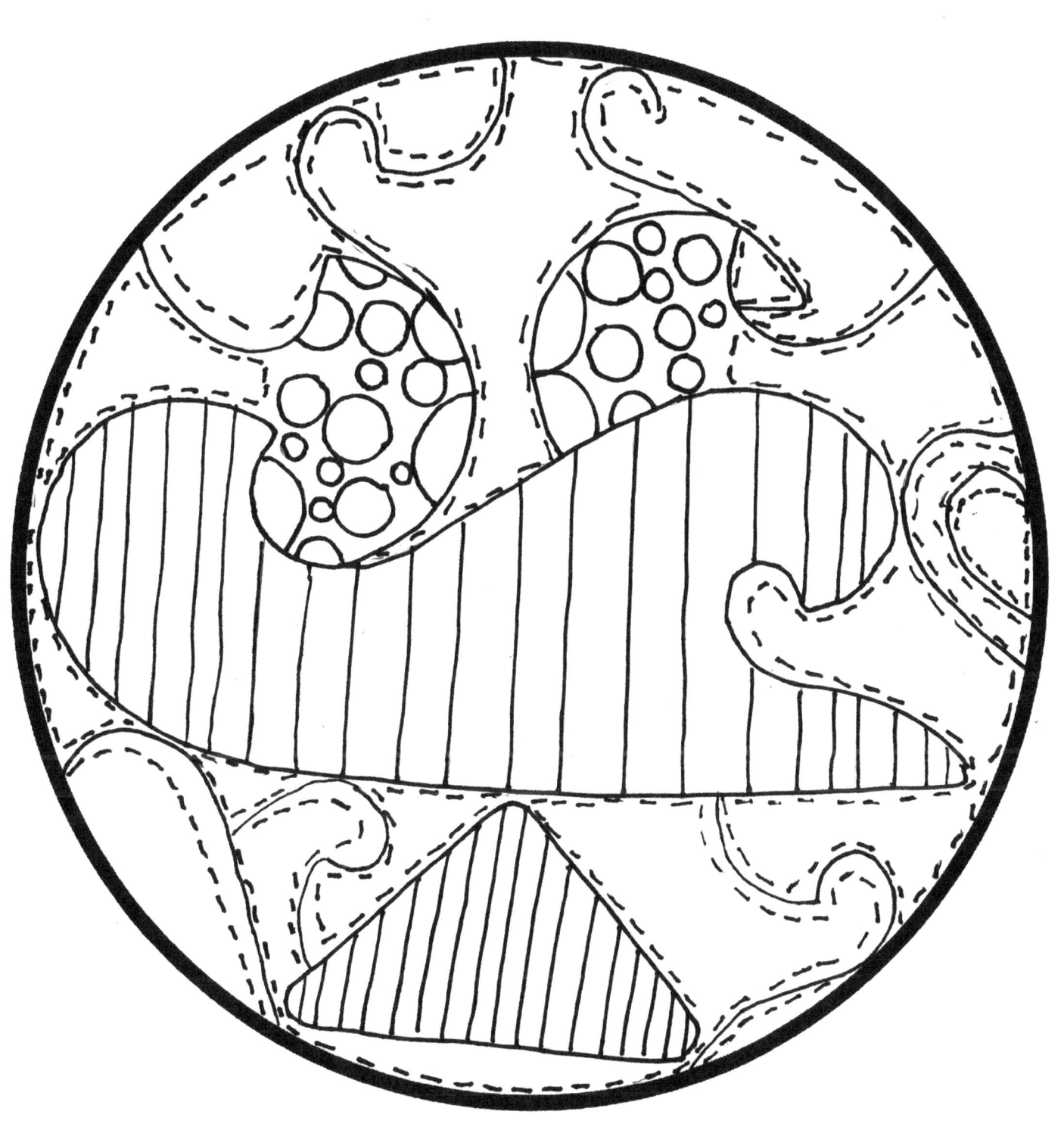

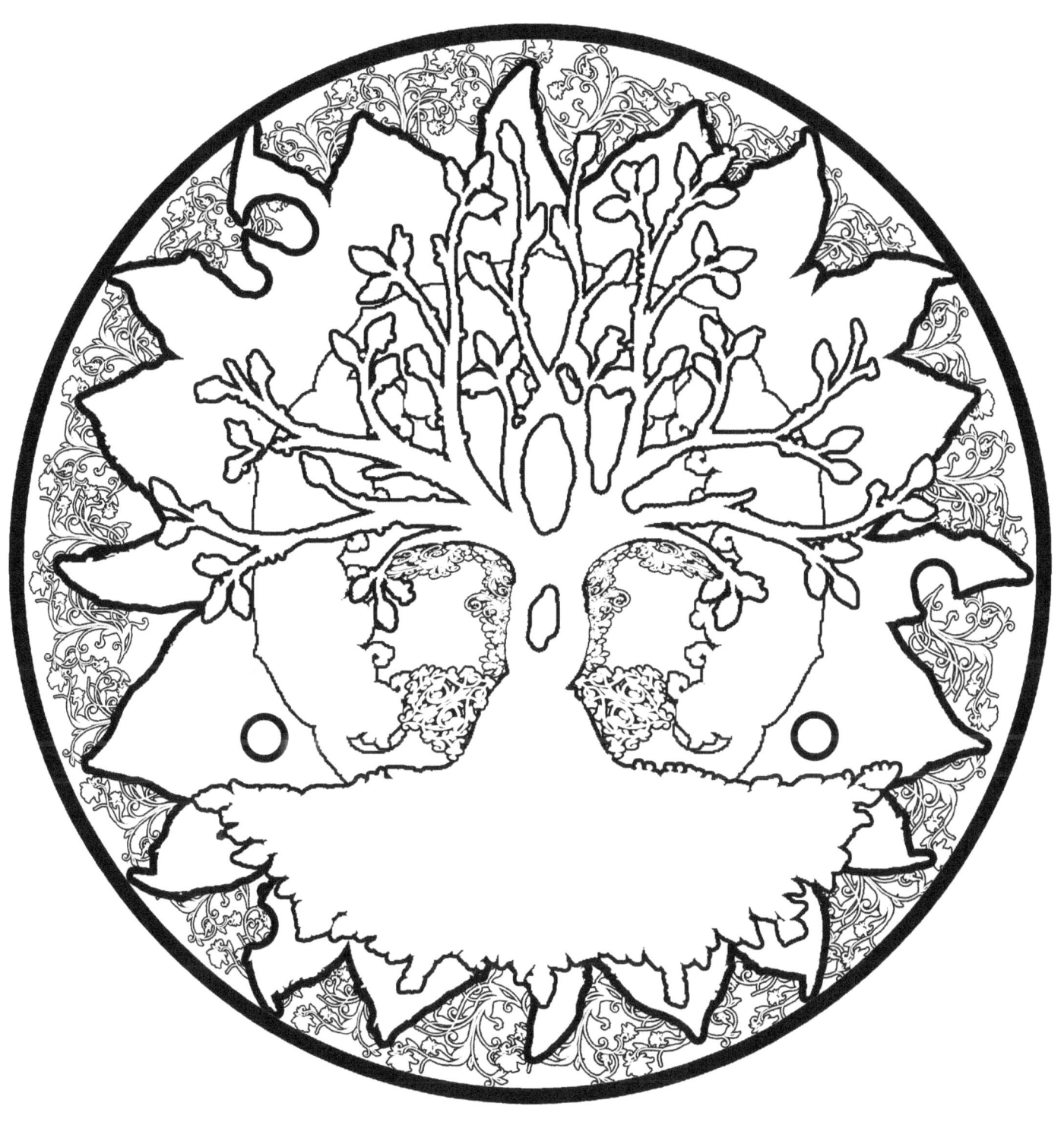

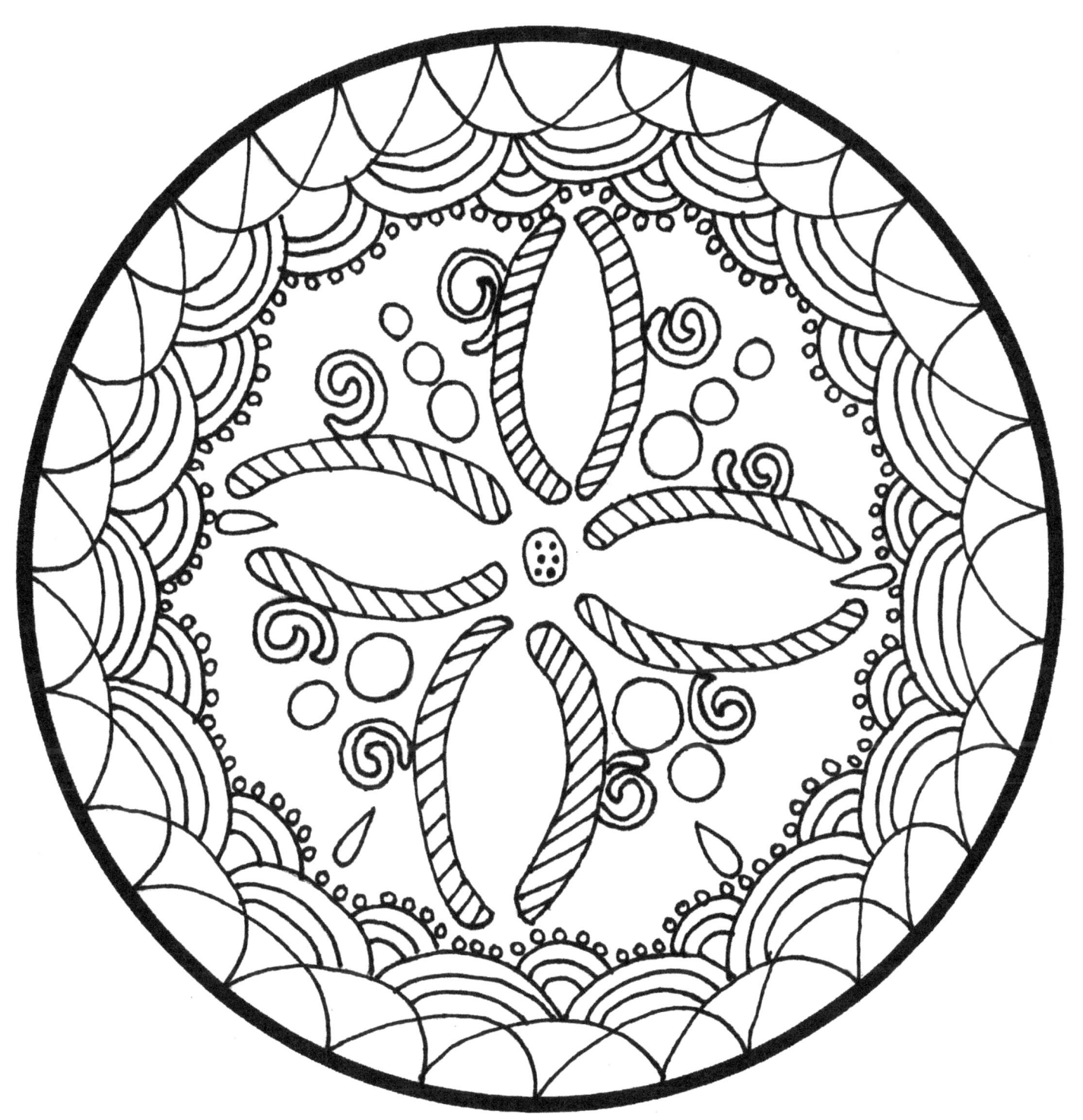

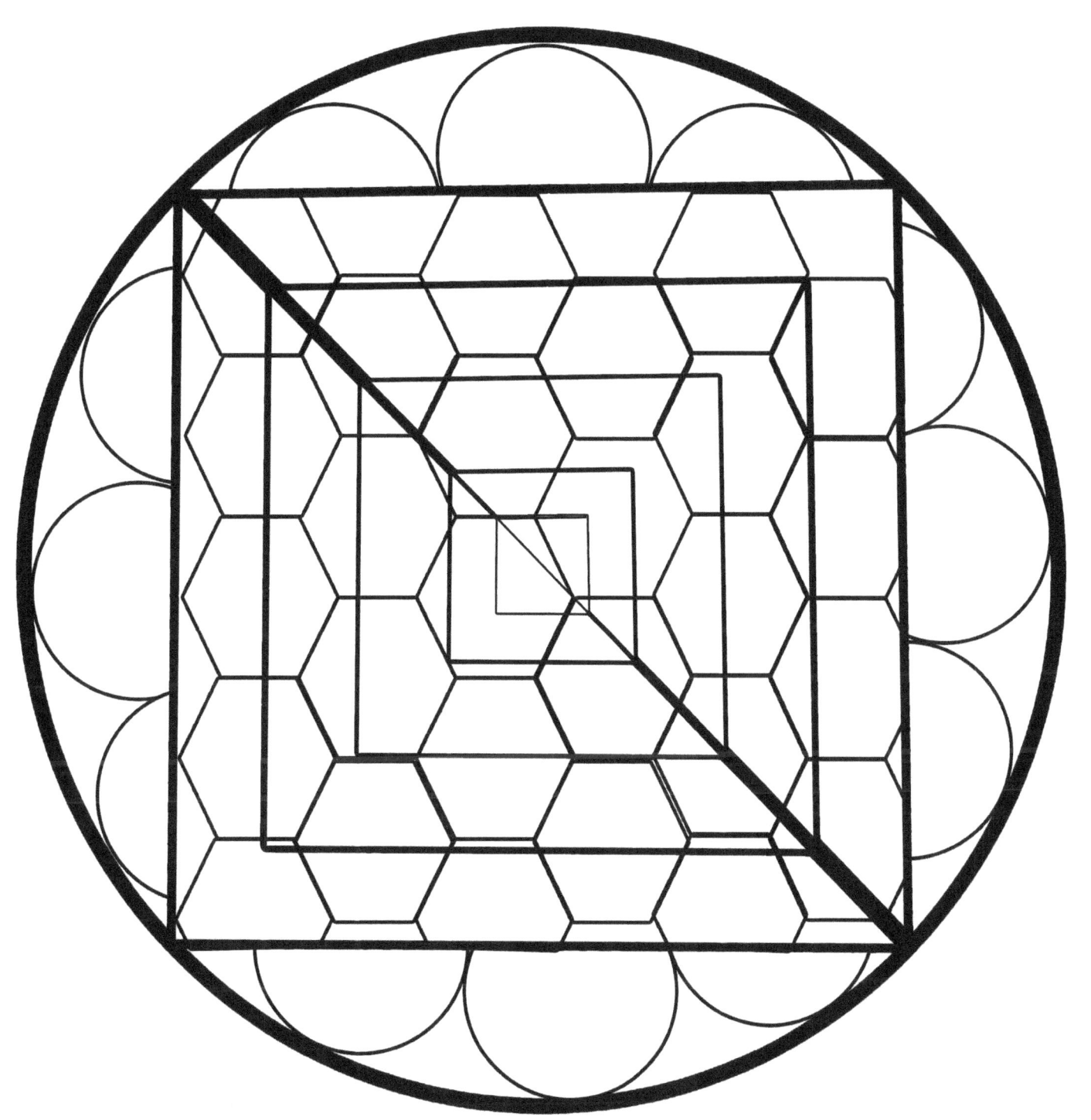

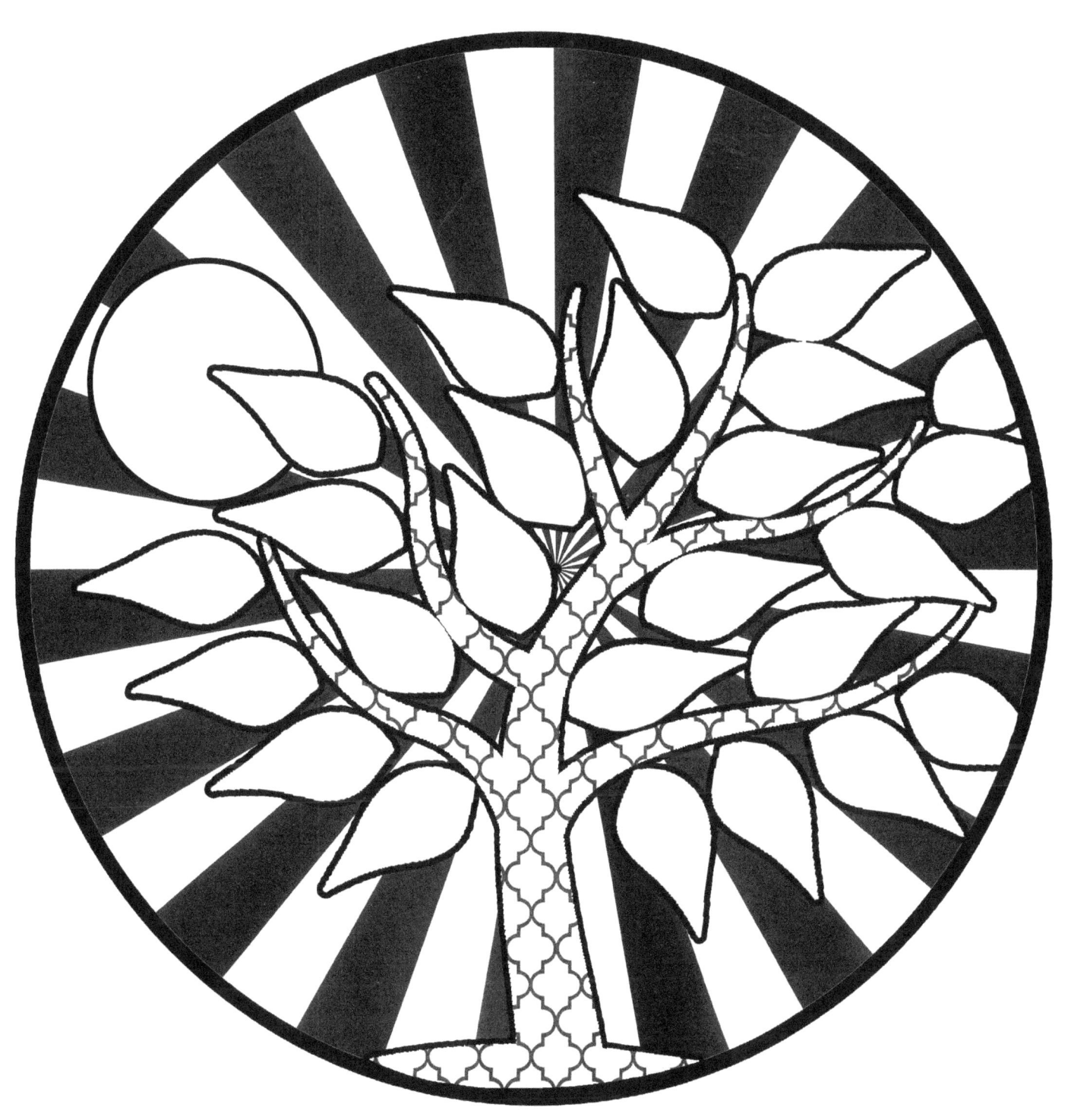

# DRAWINGPAD

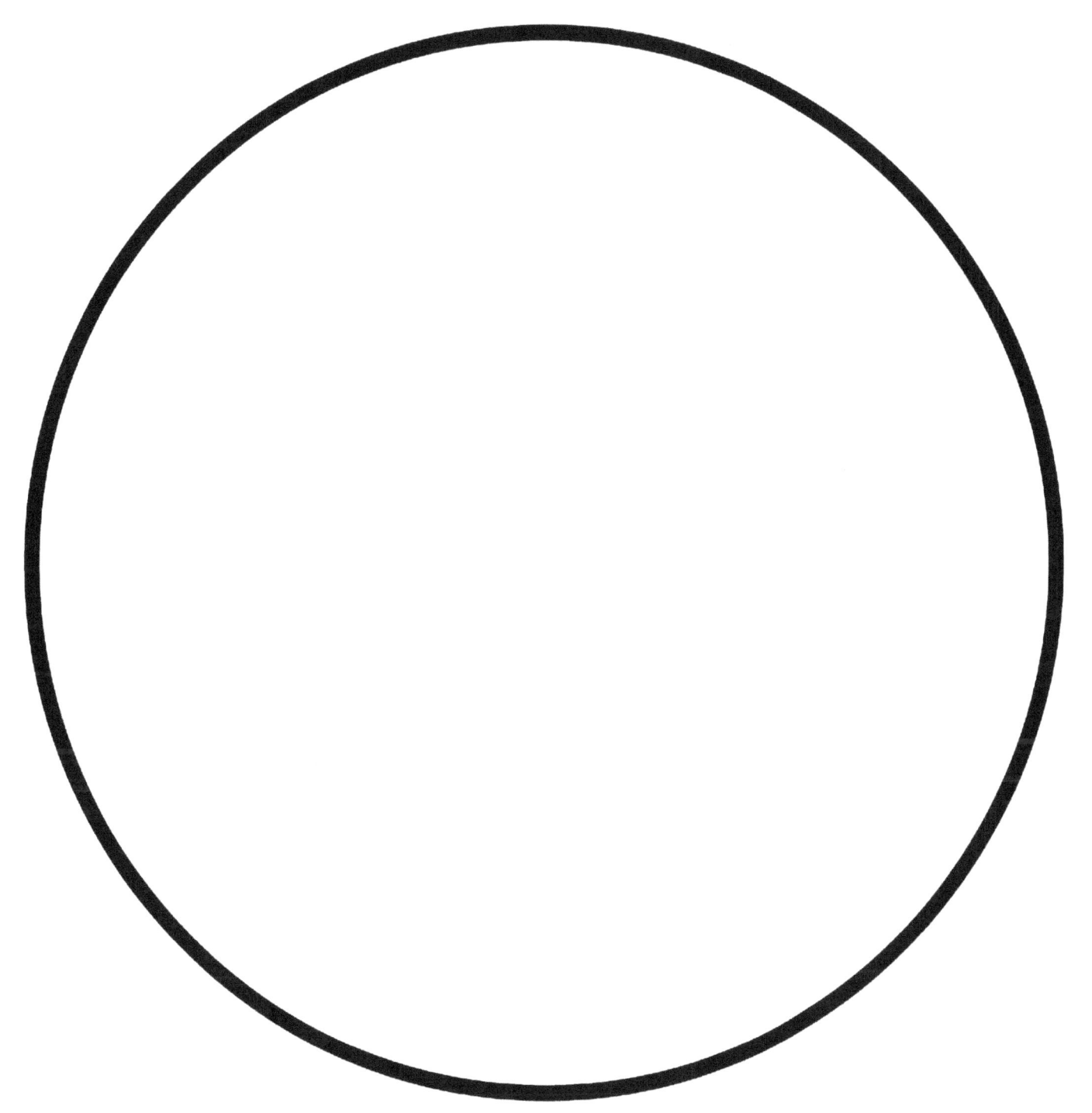

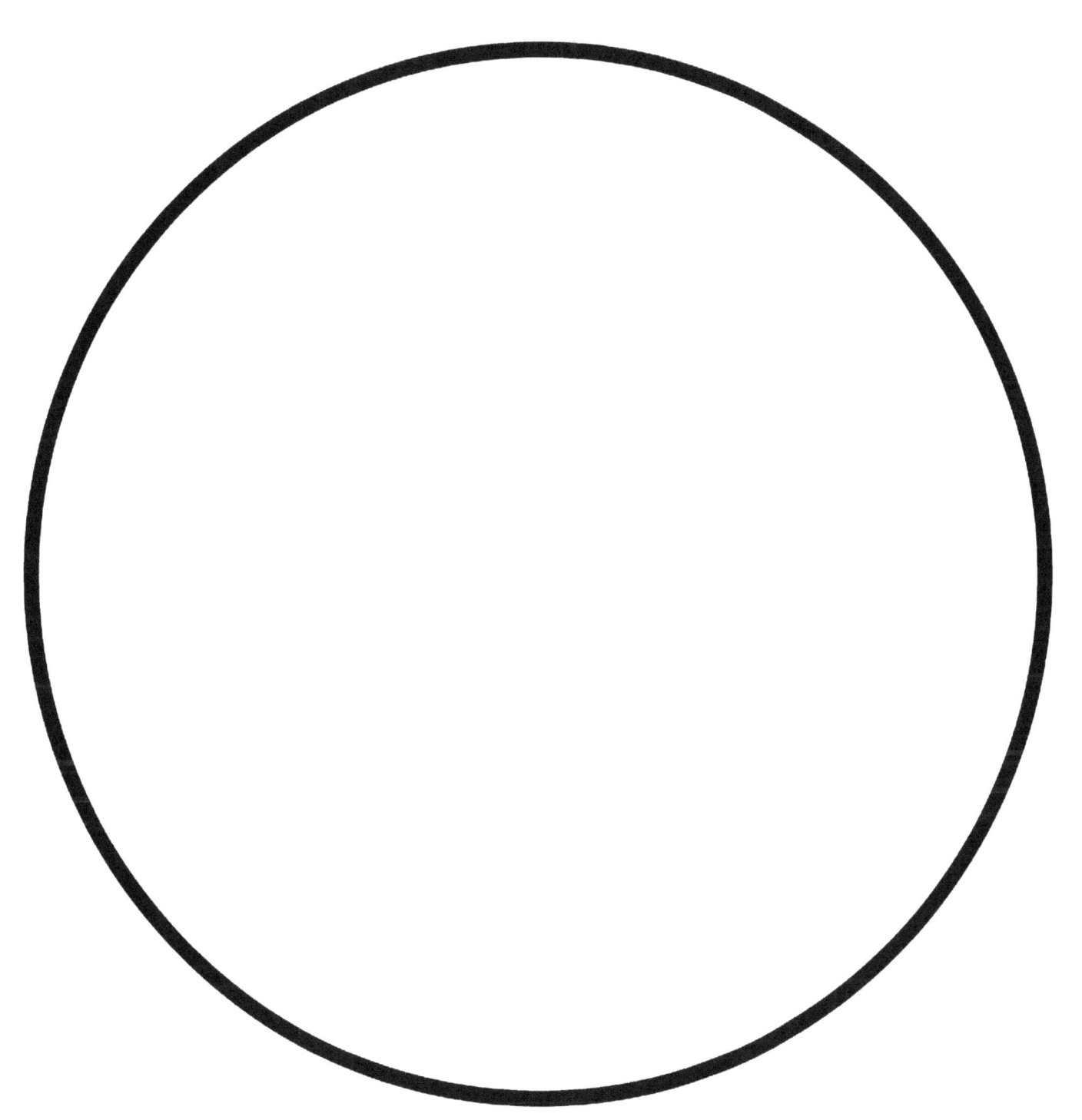

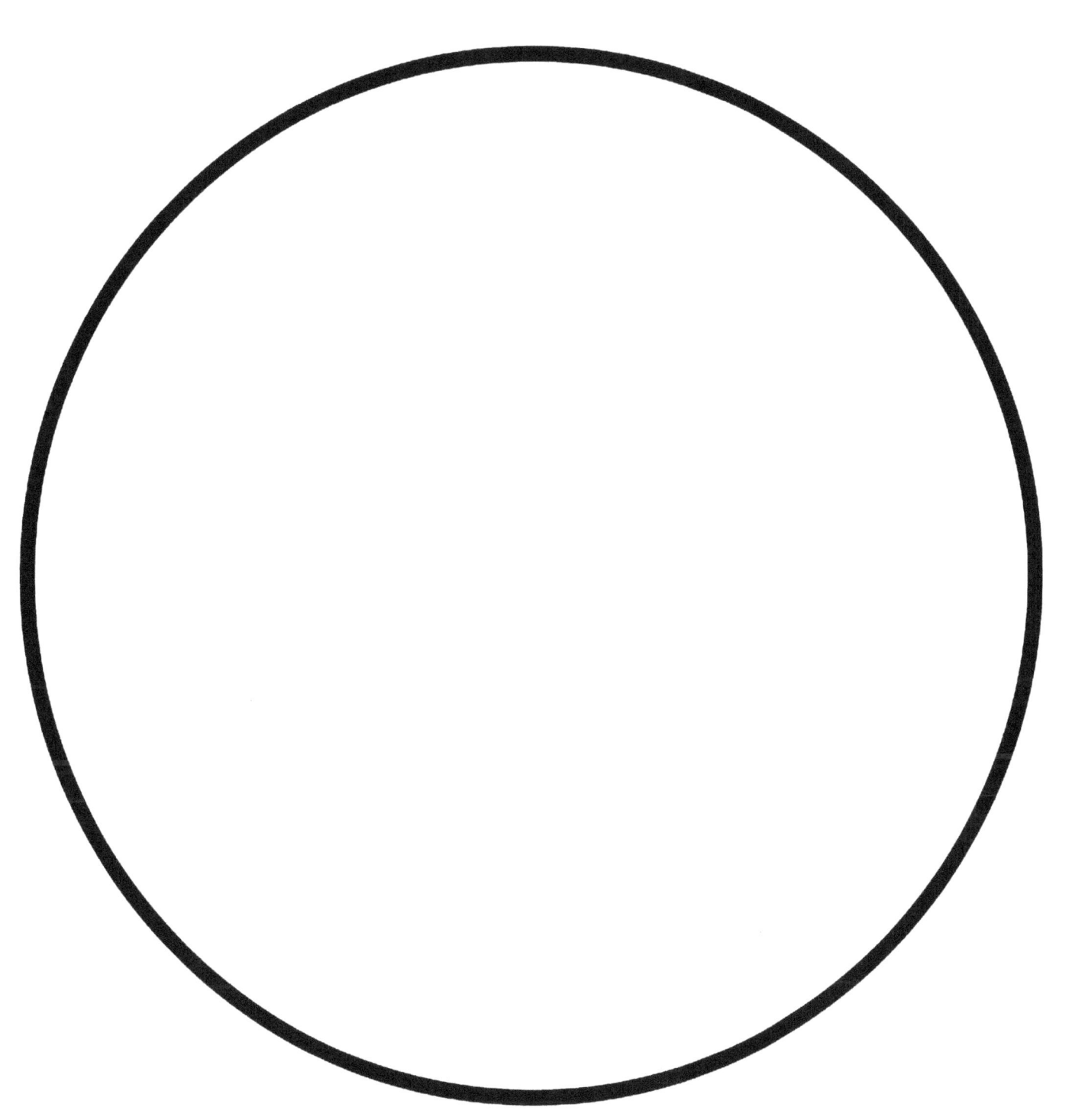

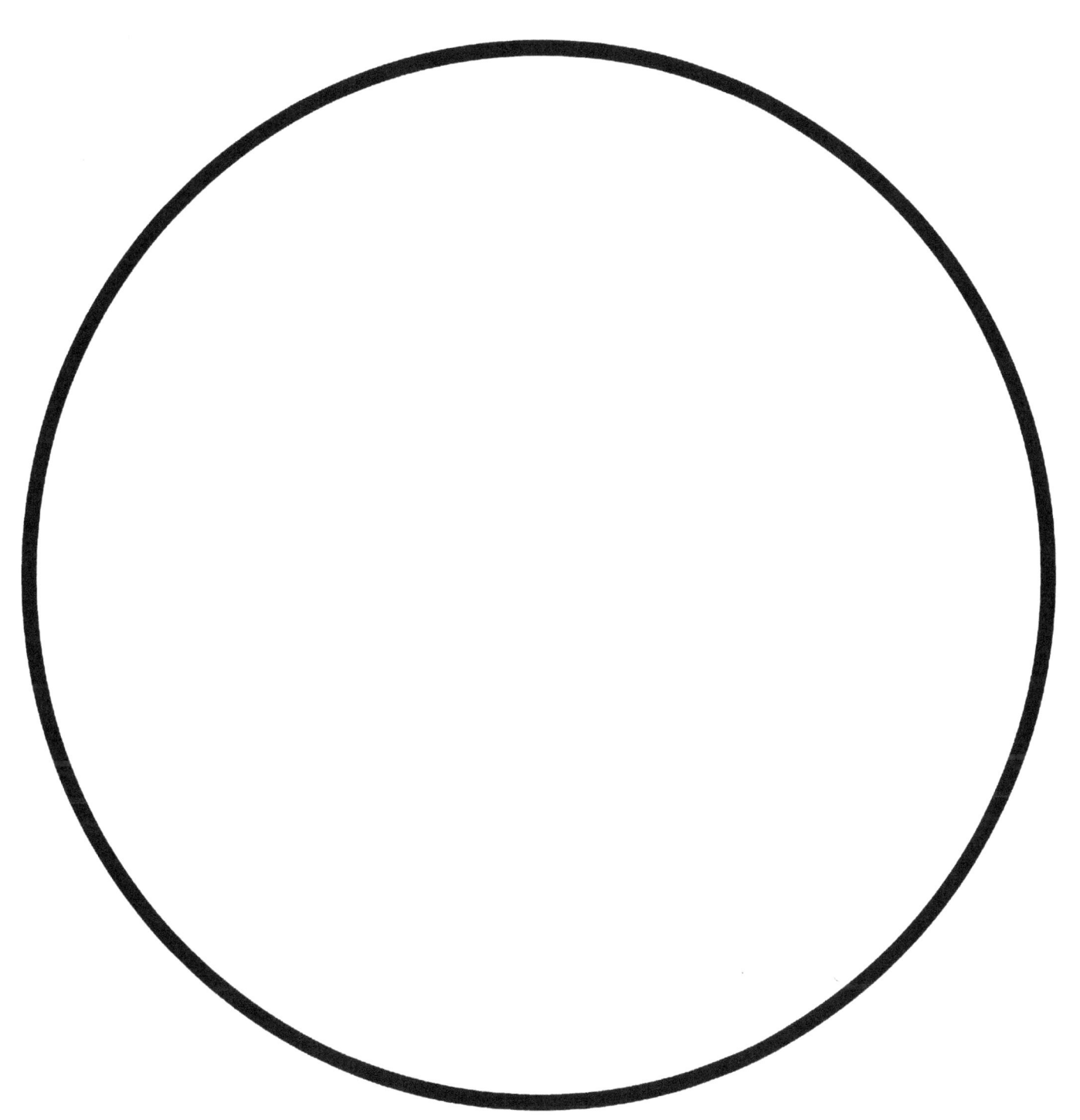

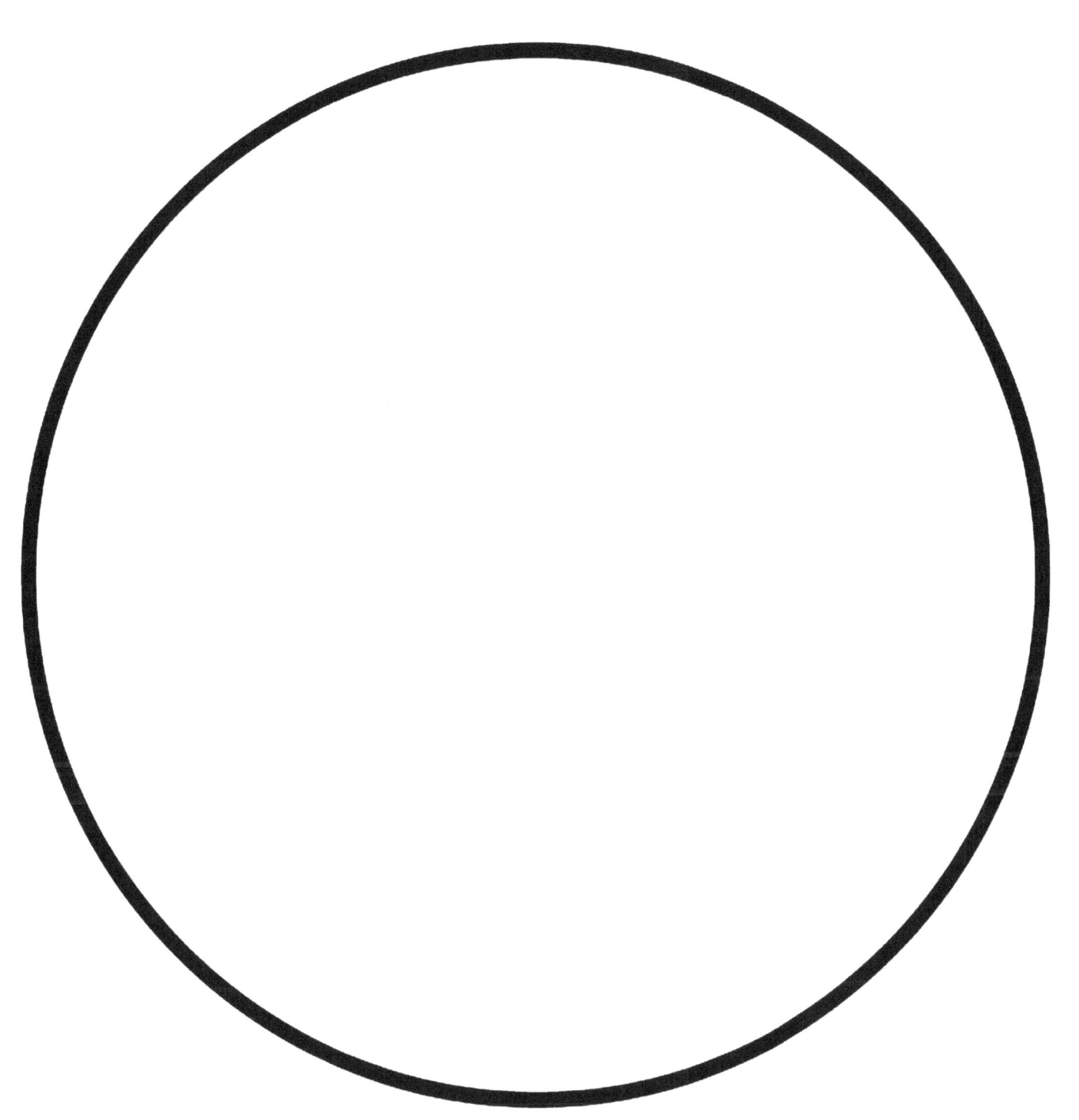

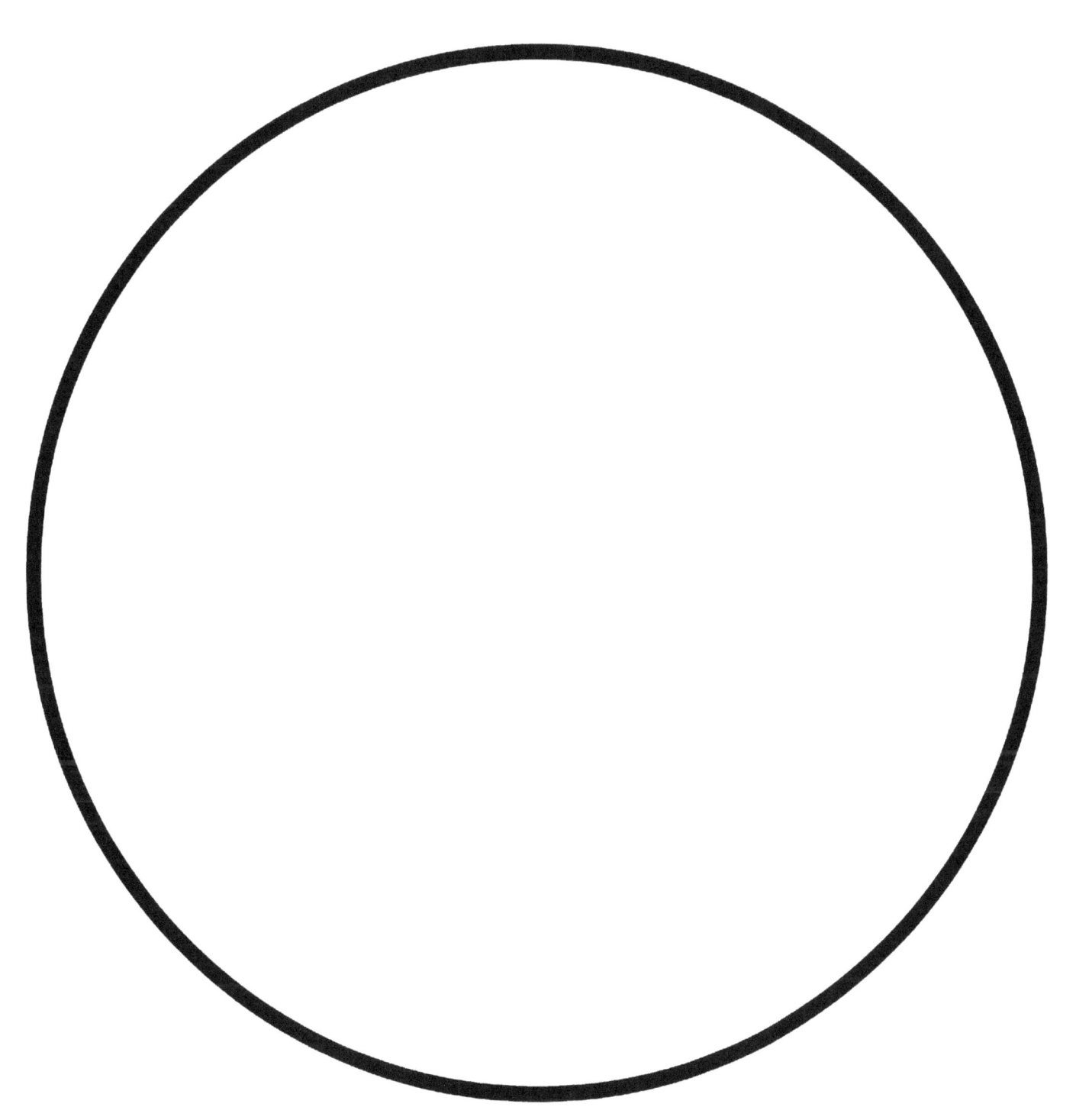

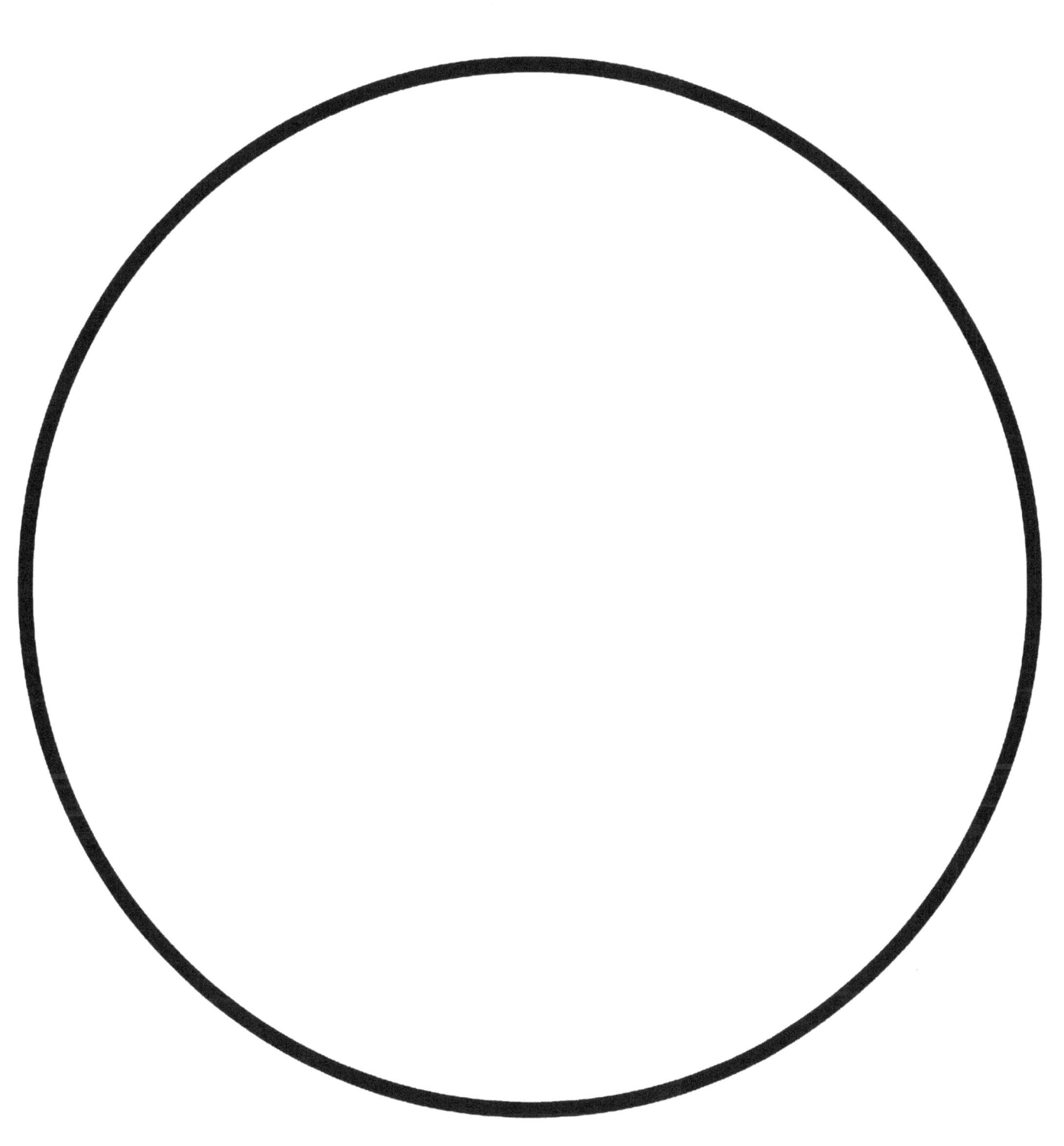

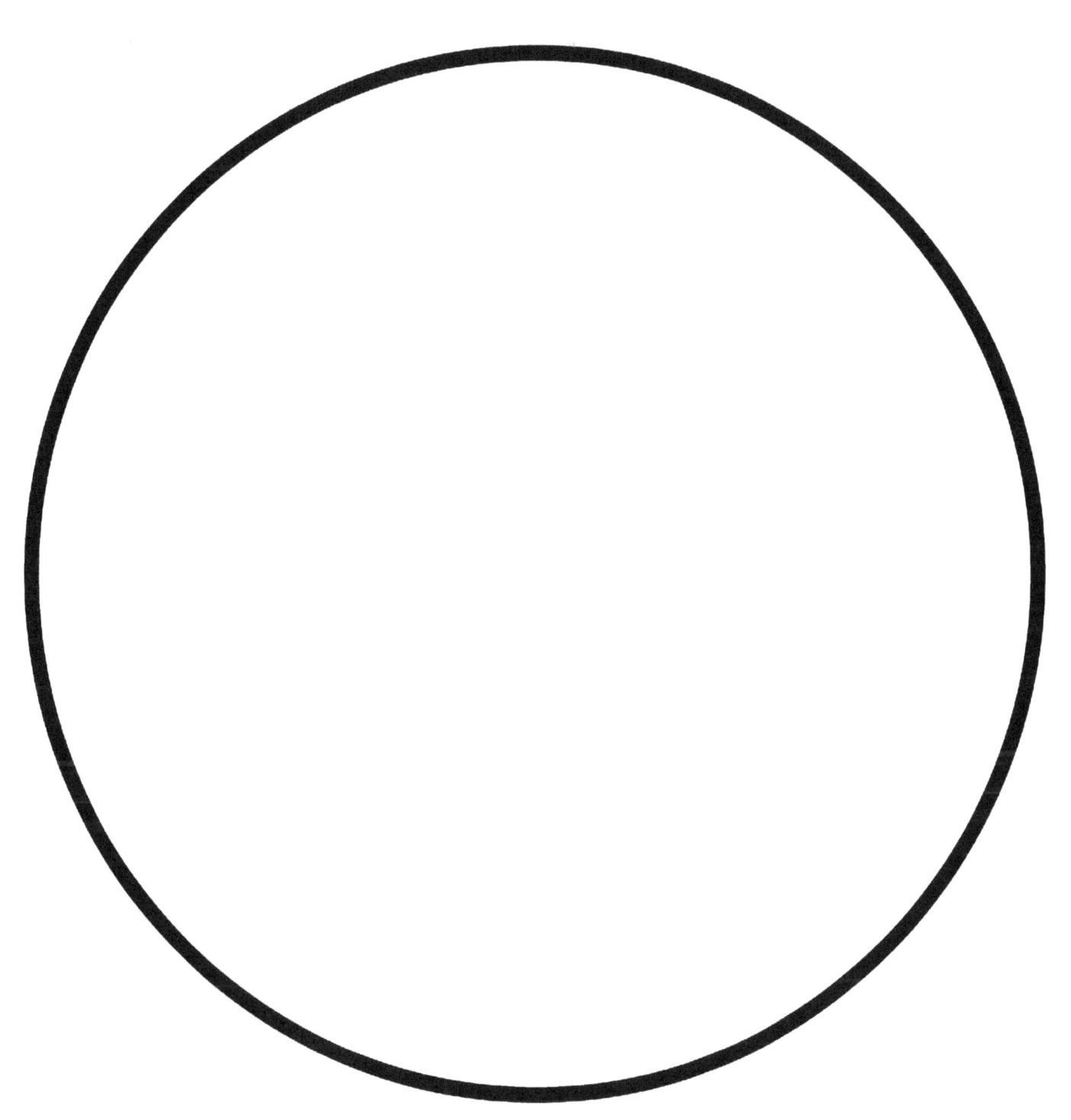

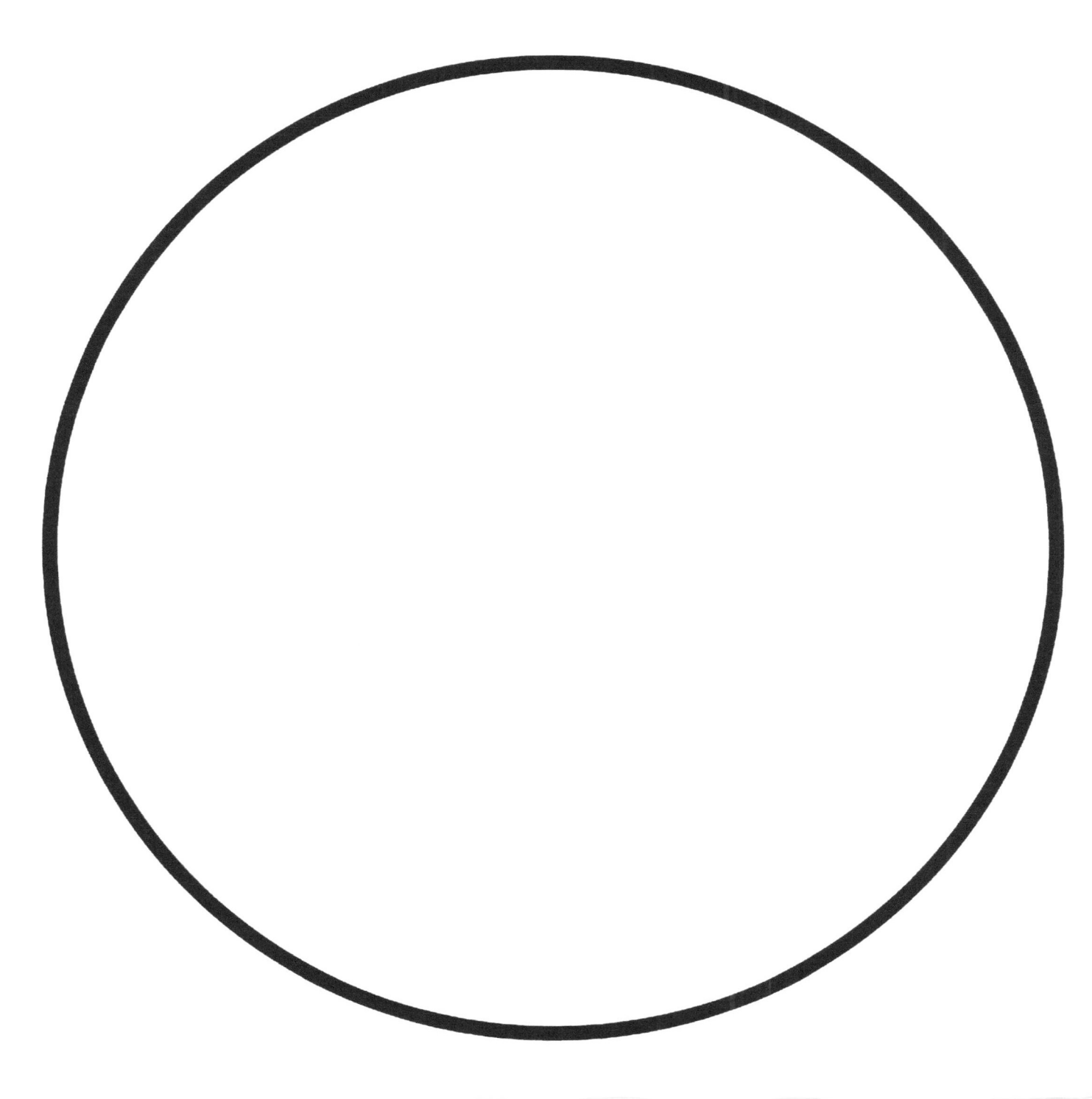

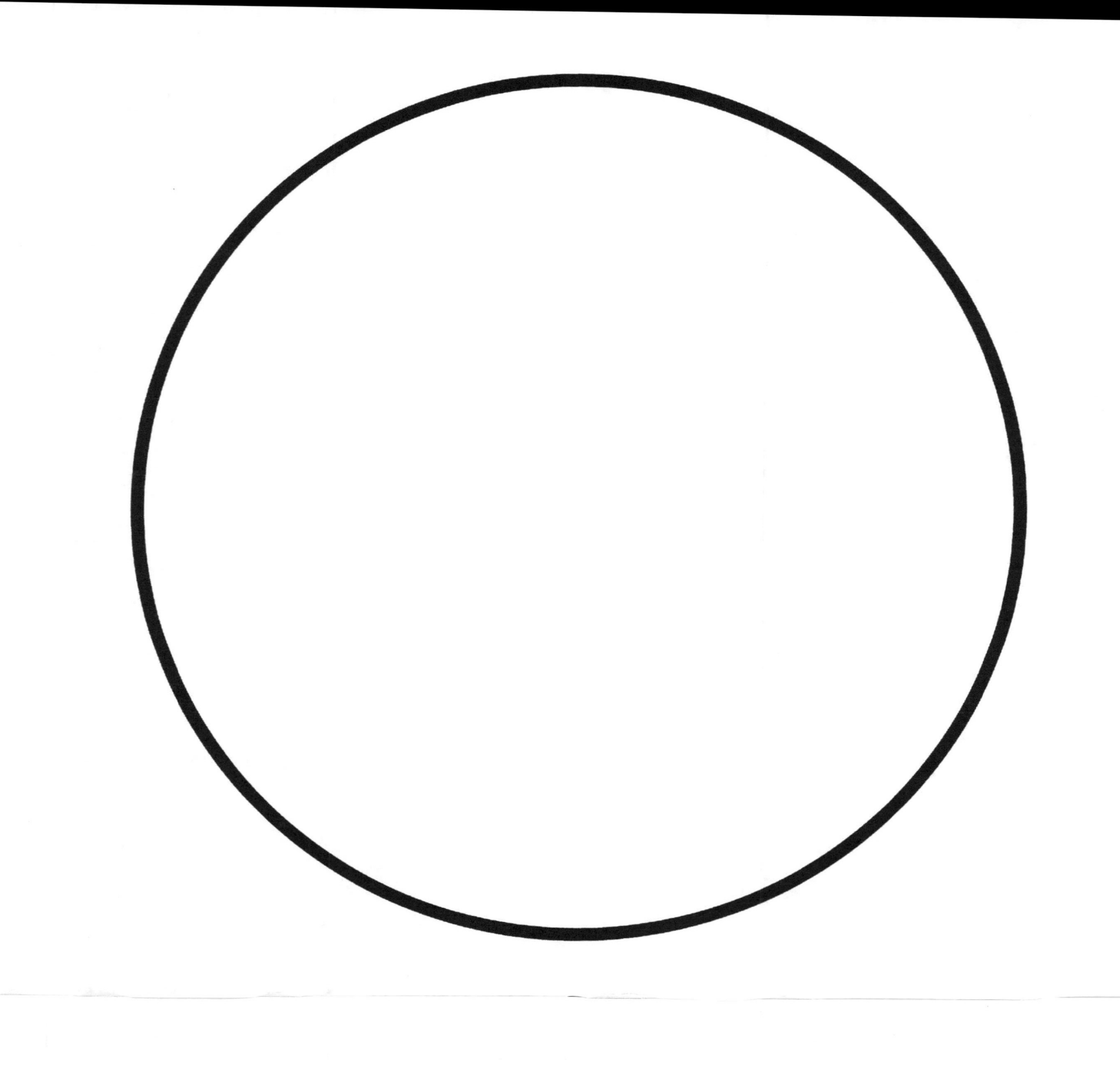